Y0-CCO-857

300
NEW WAYS
TO GET A
BETTER JOB

300 NEW WAYS TO GET A BETTER JOB

ELEANOR BALDWIN

BOB ADAMS, INC.
PUBLISHERS
Holbrook, Massachusetts

Copyright ©1991, Eleanor Rogers Baldwin. All rights reserved.
This book, or parts thereof, may not be reproduced in any form without
permission from the publisher; exceptions are made for brief excerpts used in
published reviews.

ISBN: 1-55850-016-2

Published by Bob Adams, Inc.
260 Center Street
Holbrook, Massachusetts 02343

Manufactured in the United States of America.

D   E   F   G   H   I   J

This publication is designed to provide accurate and authoritative information with regard
to the subject matter covered. It is sold with the understanding that the publisher is not engaged in rendering legal, accounting, or other professional advice. If legal advice or other
expert assistance is required, the services of a competent professional person should be
sought.

—From a *Declaration of Principles* jointly adopted by a
Committee of the American Bar Association and a
Committee of Publishers and Associations

COVER DESIGN: Peter Gouck

This book is available at quantity discounts for bulk purchases.
For information, call 1-800-872-5627.

Dedication

To many who have given support above and beyond: Norma and Lou Tornabene and Ann and Fred Davies because they always cheered my achievements and ignored my failures; Jeffrey and Glenn Baldwin, my sons, from whom I've learned so much; Ray Baldwin, the love of my life; Lee Hoffman and Lloyd Jones, for their friendly professional counsel.

—ERB

Table of Contents

Chapter 1

Welcome to the Twenty-first Century

If I called your employer in five years and asked for you, there's at least a 50 percent chance you wouldn't be there. The number one worry of Americans today is Jobs—well before their concern with drugs, crime, inflation, the trade deficit, or the environment.

This is a book that will help you keep that paycheck coming in whether you are sixty, fifty, forty, thirty, or entry level. You'll learn the street smarts that will turn you into an effective job hunter. More important, you will also begin to understand and become more realistic about why we have to seek work more often today than people did in the past.

If you are like most of us, you've been planning your future based on what you have learned from the past, from all of your previous experiences. The problem is, these allegedly time-tested techniques just don't work in today's job market.

We are in a major shift from one age to another. We have left the Industrial Age. It isn't even the year 2000 yet, but we are already living in a new era: the Information Age. Welcome to the twenty-first century!

In this new era the one sure thing is *change*. Consider these facts:

- ⬛ *One in ten of us already loses our job every year*—more and more often for reasons over which we have absolutely no control. Corporate mergers, bankruptcies, leveraged buyouts, and all the other major shakeups mean the womb-to-tomb job—lifetime employment by one company—is as outdated as yesterday's newspaper.

- ⬛ *Control of our own time has become a major issue in American society.* Priorities are being rearranged. Yet far too many employers are unaware of how this is already affecting their business. Or they are using Band-Aid treatments instead of developing comprehensive solutions that respond to the cause of this trend.

- ⬛ *The fastest-growing educational system in the United States is corporate training.* It's unfortunate for all of us that the quality of U.S. public education has failed to keep up with corporate demands for trained intellects. But at least *companies* are realizing that to regain a competitive edge in a global economy they have to compensate for the educational system's problems.

- ⬛ *It's become fashionable to be middle-aged.* That's good news to those of us who remember the phrase "Don't trust anyone over thirty." But this change has happened because most of the people who *used* to say that are now over thirty and pushing middle age themselves! As the largest single segment of the U.S. population, the so-called baby boomers (those born between World War II and the advent of the Pill in

1962) are indeed a force to be reckoned with. And they again are affecting the way all of us view our lives.

- *Retirement as we have known it is beginning to disappear.* I have no doubt that within the next decade or two a period of total leisure for perfectly healthy people age sixty-five or older will be as unusual as a husband and wife bringing in only one paycheck is today. The reasons are economic. Only this time the root cause will be the country's (rather than the family's) economic situation. Social Security can't possibly afford to pay for a life of leisure for all those physically able to perform. And many of those people won't be the least bit interested in spending all of their time sitting around watching television.

So: work life is changing. Education is changing. Lifestyles are changing. Retirement is changing. And attitudes are changing. Scary, isn't it?

It needn't be. It can be fun. And it certainly is a challenge.

The first thing you probably want to know is how all this change affects you—particularly your job decisions. How can you respond to this new era in ways that will work for you?

Whether you are an employer or an employee, you have to know what's happening in order to plan your next steps successfully. You can no longer sit back and react to things as they happen.

To be successful in this new era, both employees and those without jobs must learn new, nontraditional approaches for getting a better job. The old techniques for staying with a company, for moving up in a company, for *receiving a paycheck at all*, simply do not work in this new era.

But all of this change also means that you now have an opportunity to embark on a new adventure. You have a chance to open your mind, to try new things, to look at the world with a fresh pair of eyes.

In my business as a career and employment counselor, I've found it an exciting, creative experience to uncover new ways to find rewarding work in this era. I know they work because they've worked so well for so many people—far better than any of them expected when they gave these ideas a try!

As a job doctor, I enjoy:

1. Helping people first understand and become open to change

2. Sharing with them the many innovative approaches that already have proven to increase their chances for quick success

3. Assisting them in developing sound strategies and deciding which techniques have the best chance to work in which situation

4. Spurring them into action

5. Watching them put the parts together and succeeding beyond their expectations.

Most of that we're going to do right here. Of course, you'll have to choose for yourself which techniques to try in a given situation. And I'll miss the fun of being there to applaud your success. But I'll still enjoy starting you on your way, and I'll welcome your feedback. (Write me care of the publisher.)

The 300 new ways for getting a better job outlined in these pages move from global trends to things as simple as buying a nice portfolio to keep all the pieces together. Not all of these ideas will work for you or be appropriate to your situation. But out of this huge number of proven ideas, even if you act on only a few, your chances of making it in the Information Age will be vastly increased!

 The most important job search technique of all is to *do something*! Wherever you are in today's job market, when you see the ceiling beginning to crack, why just stand around and wait for the beams to come crashing down? ∎

Chapter 2

How Global Changes Affect Your Work

Just as prior civilizations changed from nomadic to agricultural to industrial, we are involved in another major shift: into the Information Age.

Often job change decisions are forced on us by external economic changes. It seems that nearly every family today deals with layoffs, early retirement, and company failures. Nothing is simple.

Still we hold to that outmoded view of what a model career should be, and if *we* haven't followed that track and achieved specific salary and title goals, then there is something wrong with us! We still think of finding a company with a track that will help us move from position to position in an orderly manner, from entry level to retirement.

Quit dreaming. ➤

Accept radical change as the only constant.

Regularly leaving and taking new jobs has become the norm today. In this post-industrial Information Age, many changes are taking place in the economy; these changes continually dislocate the labor force.

For companies, the price of staying in business is eternal innovation. Why else would corporations shift many jobs overseas to third-world economies where labor is cheap? In the business world today, the only constant is change! It doesn't take a lifetime for a skill, craft, or profession to become obsolete anymore. Like changes in computers, what's needed today may be totally unusable tomorrow!

We have become a society that does not look toward the future, doesn't save for the future, and certainly doesn't invest in the future in terms of human resources! You, as an individual, must provide for these needs yourself. ➤

Accept that you may have to change jobs even if you are qualified to work in a "cutting edge" growth industry.

Even in high-growth areas, buyouts and bad management are just two reasons you may find yourself looking for a new job before too long. There simply is no guarantee today for that womb-to-tomb position. Make realism and self-direction your constant companions no matter what your job title is. ➤

Recognize that the bells have tolled for the education/work/ retirement sequence.

No longer can we expect to live life in three separate stages: (1) being educated, (2) going to work, and (3) retiring to a life of leisure. Just as we have seen education becoming a lifelong process, so too is work becoming a lifelong process! (But the good news is that we may already be finding ways to enjoy a *series* of retirements at different times in our lives.)

Only during this century did people compartmentalize their lives into sequential education/work/retirement phases. What we've come to think of as normal was really just another solution to problems of the times. Executive management felt they needed to remove older workers from the work force so the younger ones could find jobs. Also, because of experiences such as the Great Depression in the thirties, workers often believed that they must hold tightly to whatever job they had until retirement, even if they felt trapped.

Today it is impractical—and downright unintelligent—to divide our lives into sequential phases of education, work, and retirement. Since we are living vigorous lives and living longer, doesn't it make more sense to break with those Industrial Revolution, factory-oriented ways of looking at work, and instead mix and match the work, leisure, and education phases of our lives more pragmatically? ➤

Plan to shoulder more burdens
yourself.

Along with the demise of the womb-to-tomb job, our aging Boomers are suddenly realizing how unpredictable work and career issues really are.

They thought, for instance, they were secure in the assumption that corporations would carry the costs of their retirement and health insurance. With fewer and fewer of us being employed by such organizations, however, and given the continual restructuring process of the few that remain, that kind of security is lost.

Don't count on government or your employer to take care of you. Most companies have become so cost-conscious that they are reluctant to install new employee services like child care because it means increased overhead. Medical costs are out of sight, so employers are continually increasing their deductibles and asking for the employee to pay more of those costs. Smaller companies can't afford to pick up those costs at all[1] ➤

Realize that moving up today often means moving out of your present company.

Today, with the drastic thinning of the managerial ranks, if you do not wish to be flexible and take many lateral moves, you probably need to move out, most likely to a smaller company where your visibility and managerial potential will be greater. ➤

Plan on being out of work!

Smart workers will start saving now for multiple retirements and job entries, interim and part-time work, consulting work, owning their own companies, paced retirement, and travel and education sabbaticals as just some of the alternatives to another job or career.

Never think of selling yourself in service to a company; come up with an idea that you can use with an organization or project for a time, then leave when it is no longer mutually satisfying. Smart companies will hunt for new matches for their good project people, but the worker cannot count on staying with any one organization. As corporate structures continue to flatten, you may find your career is moving from project to project, rather than moving up the very thin corporate ladder.

In other words, a self-directed career will involve some element of job-hopping, whether you like it or not!

In fact, because of rapid turnover and the fact that one in ten of us loses our job every year, workers already are involved in a sort of revolving cyclical life with interim "retirements" supported by a working spouse or unemployment insurance as often as by company severance pay. Unfortunately, ease of mind doesn't often accompany this kind of program. And as the baby boomers go, so we all go, since they are such a mighty demographic force, for good or bad.

In addition, those youth-oriented work policies that American businesses had devised, like mandatory retirement, are beginning to blur. Just as people's social, financial, and lifestyle needs change to reflect the times, so too will the way they work.

➤

Don't blow your cool over company restructuring; keep your options open.

 Not you. Just prepare your resume and start making inquiries: you want to stay in control of your own career. That way, you'll keep your options open. Perhaps, too, it will make you relax a little if you comprehend that more than 90 percent of companies—not just yours—have restructured their organizations, their retirement and other benefits, their compensation packages, and their career ladders. Stay low-key. ➤

Look for changes in Social
Security.

Increasing longevity and changes in the worker-to-retiree ratio will, most likely, lead to changes in Social Security. It is very possible that eligibility age will be raised, benefits will be taxed, and some benefits will be eliminated for those whose financial needs are not great. Milton Friedman, the noted economist, has long advocated that Social Security should not be for the old, but for the needy. His ideas may be instituted in the near future, if only out of financial necessity. ➤

Note that the "baby bust" has begun to enter the work force.

After the Pill was introduced in the early sixties, Americans began having fewer and fewer children, until we were in a true baby bust. Even in 1990 with the Echo Boom (the Boomers' kids) in full cry, the Boomers still are not replacing themselves (it just seems like it, because there are so many women of child-bearing age).

In the long term, it will become easier and easier for everyone to find jobs as shortages of workers increase. Recent census figures indicate that there will be five million fewer eighteen to twenty-four year olds in 1995 than five years earlier. These population projections should make it easier to get a job should you decide, at any age, to take some time off and find work later on. Many observers feel that business leaders will recognize more and more the value of the older worker, mainly because the leaders are growing older themselves. ➤

Anticipate competition.

You hear jobs are plentiful. If so, why do you have so much competition in finding work? Entry-level, lower-paying jobs are going begging while those of us who are educated and skilled (and probably care enough to read this book) face colossal competition. Let's face it, it's a ditch-digger's market! ➤

Take advantage of corporate-
sponsored training.

As we've noted, the greatest growth in education is within businesses themselves! The most humane and forward-thinking companies are retraining employees in order to retain and (not coincidentally) get a better return on their human investments. Even older workers sometimes been passed over for training because of their perceived prejudice against learning new things and because of management's very real prejudice against age, usually react favorably to the opportunity to learn something new. This is often after decades of doing the same job!

But the real growth in corporate-sponsored training is directed toward keeping the lower portion of the work force technologically competent and functionally literate. Look for a big explosion in workplace literacy programs. If Americans are to stay competitive, we must have workers who can think and solve problems. ■

Chapter 3

Totally Rethinking Work

Layoffs will continue to occur frequently: we are not unique and exclusive because it happens to us. Too many people have simply stayed on too long. Too many have allowed themselves to be lulled into a sense of security, and suddenly (they think) their job collapses on them. Too many workers walk around in this new world bewildered, wishing to stay on because of inertia or (worse) to become vested. They do not see change as opening to a world full of opportunity but only bringing insecurity and broken promises.

I consider them to be doing time.

If a layoff happens to you, you are wasting your time and effort by becoming mad, upset, or hurt. You need to get out, exercise, and start *controlling your own career*. You'll love yourself in the morning for it! ➤

Make your individual career
track.

Forget all you have stored in your memory about climbing the corporate ladder; that's a carryover from womb-to-tomb thinking. The much-ballyhooed corporate career track is fast becoming a myth.

Instead, make change your ally. Understand that nothing can remain static. Your option now is to build your *own* track, one that will most probably include moving from company to company and from project to project.

Choose to find the *right* job and not the *first* job. Take the responsibility to develop your own career. And don't be afraid to change course if that's for the best! ➤

Realize that a career position is rarely if ever a nine-to-five job.

One of the major differences between the salaried and hourly employee is the willingness of the salaried worker to work the time needed to get the job done; to show initiative and the ability to see the big picture. If you're always out of the door by five, you have a clerical mentality and are, frankly, unrealistic about the weekly hours professionals work (almost forty-nine for men, a few less for women). ➤

Join the revival of the
Renaissance man or woman.

Perhaps you honestly don't aspire to management, and would prefer to work less and enjoy more leisure time. If you have planned ahead, you'll be able to forego regular paychecks for more time, and you'll be able to engage in the things you like right now. Wouldn't it be a wonderful reviver of momentum to have planned sabbaticals—a few months off here and there throughout your life to pursue special projects or to reeducate yourself? That would be a wonderful way to revitalize your interest in your major work, your family, or to retool for another career.

If you can dream it, you can plan it! ➤

Ask yourself: Who is most likely to become an entrepreneur?

The baby boomers, because they are a huge demographic block with considerable job competition, have worked long enough to have some solid experience, and have found the loss of a career track can sometimes be compensated for by becoming their own boss.

This track, however, is definitely not for everyone. If you are thinking about starting your own business, you should think long and hard about whether you are willing to:

- Work much harder than before
- Work much longer hours than before
- Put family and relationships on the back burner, at least for a time
- Secure adequate financing
- Meet a payroll (if you hire others)
- Market effectively. ➤

Fit work into life on your own terms.

While we wait for the workplace to change, it is up to us to fashion our own lifestyle around the following items:

1. **Our core of expertise.** Aptitudes (number memory, skills, spatial aptitude, logic, emotional steadiness, organizational ability); technical skills (computer entry, carpentry, mechanics); and experiences in a definitive area (cost accounting, production management, editing, counseling, fast-food management, contract negotiating, elementary teaching, photography).

2. **Our personal desires.** The time, the enjoyment, and flexibility of our work; the quality of personal life; being with family and friends. Today, many employees seek to work for companies and managers who are ethical and socially responsible.

3. **Our financial needs** for today, for the future education of our children, and also for our own old age. With the high level of job turnover now, fewer than a quarter of Americans have pension plans. Plan ahead financially for your own job interim times as well as for health and retirement finances.

4. **Our health.** Often we are not able to continue to do what we once found physically easy. One of my most challenging assignments as an employment counselor was helping a television news cameraman who loved his job to find new career direction after an injury would no longer allow him to maneuver that heavy camera.

5. Geographic location. Because of ease of communicating with computers and fax machines, many people can live and work where they wish. In fact, after decades of decline, we are now noticing a rise in the populations of smaller towns.

 Some of my private clients and friends have already started small family-owned service businesses at the same time their principal career is in full swing. Usually the whole family participates.

→ For one, it's the ownership of a retail store in a nearby bedroom community. Dad had been the principal breadwinner in another demanding career, so Mom is the person who has given most to the family business. But both their son and their daughter have worked in the management and operation of the store at some time. In fact, all have educated themselves in computer studies, accounting, and other business courses in order to meet the needs of the business.

Now, with the son and daughter grown, married, involved in their own careers, and with the major breadwinner recently retired, the store is Mom and Dad's joint venture. This insures that both can continue to be active, but they also are able to keep a less rigid schedule that will allow for frequent travel and for studies they had postponed.

→ Another younger family operates an office maintenance business two evenings a week. They hire extra help now and then, but usually do the work themselves. Though well educated, Mom and Dad consider this physical work good exercise. At present, the money earned goes toward future college expenses. Think of all the wonderful lessons their children are growing up learning—the value of the dollar, dependability (even when they don't feel like it), flexibility, and the satisfaction of a meaningful task well done. They are together as a family much more than most. The family could even decide to expand this business to become their principal source of income.

→ An attorney friend of mine is planning a total career change. With his children grown and educated, he no longer has to have a tremendous salary to support a growing family. So, in a year or so he plans to enroll in a professional photography school to fulfill a life-long interest.

→ A business associate, a counselor and college administrator, finds herself having to choose because of time pressures among three options in which she is already involved: her regular forty-hour-plus weekly administrative job, teaching, or private psychological counseling. Her decision will be guided by financial considerations, the flexibility of her full-time employers, and what she most desires to do with her time, *not* by panic for a paycheck. This is the kind of problem we should all have! ➤

Realize there are advantages to
being older.

Ready for a surprise? Younger workers consistently have more sick days per year than older ones do. The unhealthy older workers have already opted out of the system. And in this post-industrial economy, fewer jobs are physically demanding, but more are intellectually so. It is an awful waste of our national treasures—an experienced and dedicated work force—to throw away all this wisdom because someone reaches "retirement" age.

Many companies have realized this and are employing their treasures part time—to retain contacts, to keep them from being hired away by the competition, to fill in during demanding periods, or to offer invaluable experience which has grown out of a lifetime career. American companies are already being forced to rely on the sharpened experience of age, mixing it with the energy and ambition of the young.

For financial and psychological reasons, many people today are questioning the wisdom of full retirement at *any* age—not only because of issues of personal fulfillment, but also because businesses are finding that they have thrown away many irreplaceable skills and cooperative people with a strong work ethic. Later middle age is rapidly becoming a time when people don't stop work and completely retire; they often stay on full time or become contract, seasonal, consulting, or part-time employees.

➤

Accept responsibility and

control of your career.

We all want to be able to blend our own mixture of work and hobby, consulting and travel. Some lucky people control how they use their own time today, long before they may have reached upper middle age. In order to emulate them, we must learn self-control and personal responsibility—and that means developing time management, personal finance and saving, stress management, self-promotion, and job hunting skills. In the later how-to chapters of this book, you'll find outlined suggestions on how to use all these facets of personal control. ➤

Plan knowing that retirement as we know it will disappear.

Already some people accept the thought of retirement happily, especially if their work is physically demanding and not intellectually stimulating. Perhaps their workplace is populated with unpleasant people!

But almost half of today's retirees feel a need to explore and find usefulness in a life that for too long has been tied simply to one career or area of expertise. Especially for males who are acculturated to work, who have *become* their job, their whole sense of self-worth is tied to it. No job, no self-worth.

You are going to be a person for as long as you live. If being a productive, employed person is part of what makes you happy, you should know that you will not be alone if you opt to continue a career well past what we once considered "retirement age." ➤

Counteract barriers to finding alternative jobs.

These barriers are part of the old womb-to-tomb mentality.

Employers wanting us to work full-time are a definite barrier to the job flexibility that many people, especially women and older workers, would like to see. Women with small children and most older employees would like to control of their time. Without stopping work altogether, they would like employers to offer flextime, consulting, or part-time work options.

In addition, older workers are often viewed, sometimes with no good reason, as old dogs who cannot learn new tricks, rigid and unwilling. Many prospective employees think they cannot start a new career or education after age forty, fifty-five, or sixty. But, because finances must be supplemented (after all, we live much longer nowadays!) paying our way becomes a problem if we do not consider continuing to work.

Despite federal laws, real age discrimination on the part of employers will diminish only as the Boomers themselves grow older. ➤

Emulate outstanding examples of
valued older workers.

I know a man who has successfully retired from three professional jobs. One of our ministers has just announced his third retirement (or maybe his fourth). Another friend has retired from two jobs and now serves actively on a city planning board. Another has been nursing, full- and part-time, for the last fifty-four years! (I noticed at a social gathering recently that she was the one up getting coffee for everyone, too. In taking care of everyone else, she has kept herself vital and healthy.)

Common sense tells me that all these super people have to be in their seventies. But they don't think of themselves as old in any accepted sense of the word. Men and women like these are wonderful treasures; ignoring them would be a terrible loss to any community. Employment trends suggest baby boomers will bring this "Renaissance career approach" to full flower. ➤

Realize that job burnout now usually occurs around age thirty-seven.

Because of the frantic pace of life today, the fast track loses its appeal at a younger age than ever before. Thirty-seven has become the average age of those ready to trade that fast track for more personal fulfillment and time with friends and family. In other words, workers at this age start to question total absorption in one's job. (Interestingly, I see more professional men than women with this problem.)

Unfortunately, just as individual workers are feeling they want more time for themselves, employers are slimming down staffs and piling on ever-heavier workloads. As the tasks grow, professionals must learn to delegate to others at work and at home. Since they are spread so thin, they must empower others to take up some of the slack. Some personalities, however, have a great deal of trouble letting go of responsibilities . . . enter burnout. ➤

Don't panic: feel free to suggest new options to employers.

It is up to each of us to educate America's employers to our desires, at all ages, for more flexible work/play/study arrangements. Workers with small children need job flexibility most of all. Older workers want it too. As the market for good-quality employees tightens because of the low birth rates, employers will be forced to negotiate a "cafeteria" of work options and benefits as broad as today's "cafeteria" of health plans. ➤

Know that interviewers are going to have to be more flexibly results-oriented.

Perhaps more difficult is the task of convincing lower-level personnel and human resource people that they should be more flexible about hiring people who can *do* the job. These guardians must get over their fetish with dates worked and immediate insistence on salary histories. Many an interviewer shoots himself in the foot today because of this rigid, out-of-date, and irrelevant thinking. ➤

Accept that it is your responsibility to convince the interviewer that your skills are applicable.

The burden of convincing a potential employer that the skills developed in one industry or business are applicable to another rests on you, the lonely job hunter. You must learn to speak the language of the new industry, while selling yourself as a person who is not tied to rigid thinking and who will bring fresh ideas, profitable skills, and new applications.

The real solution here has to do with the terms under which "unproven" workers are hired. I think you'll find that pay will be increasingly tied to performance in the form of bonuses. This gives workers a sense that they control their own earnings, and it helps the employer control costs. ➤

Pay attention to the jargon used within your target industry.

If you're trying to break into a new area, become familiar with the special language used in that business. Read trade journals. Ask friends or benefactors who know the industry to explain unfamiliar terms. Knowing the right words to use is part of the "cloning" process will be discussing in detail later on.

Hit the library stacks! Read up on your target industry! ➤

Find out whether an MBA is worth achieving.

"Should I get an MBA?"

This is a question that I hear most often from technical clients who see their progress impeded, if not totally cut off, because of that totally technical background. I certainly do not recommend going straight from college to business school. Real world experience will make business school more valuable.

First, do a little research before taking the plunge. You'll find that MBAs tend to hire MBAs, especially for executive positions. Certain jobs, especially in financial areas, require one. But the MBA is one of those snob degrees, so you'll have to try your hardest to attend one of the top schools, such as Stanford, Harvard, or Wharton.

Lastly, realize that more jobs are in smaller companies where the emphasis is on results, not necessarily credentials. To these companies your MBA will often just make you look expensive. So target your companies and do some calling for advice to executives in those businesses before making your decision.

In other words, find out if there are jobs available that you would like once you have that degree. Remember, it's always easy to be a student; sometimes it is very hard to find work afterwards. ∎

Chapter 4

Handling Life's Accelerating Tempo

Remember Robin Williams in the movie *Moscow on the Hudson*? He played a Russian defector who was sent to a U.S. supermarket by his host family to buy coffee. Instead of the usual long food lines he was accustomed to back home in Moscow, he found the multiple choices among coffees so overwhelming that he fainted from outright culture shock.

We may not faint away, but these life and job choices take their gradual toll on our peace of mind. We feel guilty when we just sit and watch the clouds in the sky or the water lapping by a lake.

As we adjust to the realities of the two-career household, the decision to have children later in life and of the demographic pressures, we must also accept that the overall tempo of life has picked up dramatically. How to handle the various stresses is the focus of this part of the book. ➤

Understand the mass psychology of a declining job market—so you won't get caught in it.

We are in an era of rapid geographic dislocation. What that means is Boston is up while Dallas is down, or California is up while New York is down—or the opposite.

When we live in a geographic area with high unemployment, our mind disregards the good news and singles out instances that prove how awful things really are. I'm here to tell you that I have clients who have gotten jobs in the Texas down economy although they were too old, too young, in real estate or oil, and/or physically crippled. All, however, fought *against* getting caught up in the downward psychological spiral that always occurs when high expectations are brought back to earth with a resounding thud. If you'll look at the statistics, they usually aren't nearly as bad as you'd think they should be for all the gloom you hear.

Brooding can become a self-fulfilling prophecy. We can drop into depression. (Symptoms of clinical depression are lethargy, having trouble sleeping or sleeping too long, low self-esteem, compulsive behavior, avoiding solving problems, poor eating habits, and desperation.)

Think flexibly. Get out and exercise. Listen to motivational tapes. Organize your day and strike off small items concluded. Finally, stay away from gloomy people! ➤

Learn to emotionally accept
change.

Too often, we carry around outmoded thinking patterns and ideas that prevent us from easily accepting change.

These emotionally upsetting thoughts range from the idea that conflict and differences are wrong to the idea that we are controlled by external circumstances and have little or no control over what happens to us. Women in particular have been struggling to conquer various unproductive patterns: the desire to be loved or approved by everyone, the need to be dependent on others and have someone stronger to lean on, as well as the attempt to be all things to all people—filling everyone's needs but one's own.

Some people believe that past history has set present behavior, which totally precludes change! Don't succumb to such negative self-talk. Take control and change your world for the better. ➤

Decide what expertise you have to sell.

Let's face it: it is impossible to know everything today. What we have to sell to an employer in the Information Age is expert information. But no one person could possibly know all there is to know—even on one given subject—because of the boom in knowledge brought about by the computer. (Experts say that ninety-five percent of the scientists who ever lived are alive today!) But since we can't know cold what we feel we *need* to know cold, many of us remain frozen in our tracks.

Particularly among detail-oriented persons, there is such a need to do everything the right way (which usually means doing it the traditional way) that they end up doing nothing at all rather than make a mistake. They do not manage their careers, but wait until they've been fired, laid off, or demoted to consider career options. Then they force themselves through the agony of job hunting while unemployed or when their self-confidence is at its lowest. Some of these workers actually end up on the streets.

These people still think in sequential education/work/retirement life phases. They believe there is still a job track. They may even use old-style resume-driven job hunt tactics. Don't be one of them! Isolate your special area of expertise. ➤

Before resigning your present job, think about making several lateral moves within your organization in order to gain the expertise to be valuable in smaller, results-oriented companies.

In other words, learn many things so you will have the built-in flexibility to fill whatever needs your organization might require. Employers often define an employee worth keeping as one that they can count on to happily learn a new job and to do it reasonably well within a short period of time. ➤

Become a responsible job seeker.

The wise job-seeker affirms the new value system of self-control of job, health, and emotions. These people put self-direction and meaningful satisfaction (with the job and with themselves) ahead of money and total self-sacrifice to the desires of their employer. That does not mean they are lazy and do not work hard. By the same token, they don't go overboard and believe that they are wholly self-sufficient and should not ask others for help; ultimately everything happens through people.

These self-directed workers have often had negative personal job experiences just as you may be facing. However, they are results-oriented and self-driven and rightly reason that since an employer is very likely not to be able to be loyal to them in the midst of all the business mergers, failures, restructurings, and acquisitions, then they, the workers, will not be foolishly self-sacrificing, but will take control of what is best for them as an individual. This is the profile of the successful worker that is emerging as we approach the new century. ➤

Take responsibility for your education.

There is a tremendous market for continuing education, seminars, and self-help materials of all kinds. I have noticed in the years I've been speaking and training that the seminars that have grown most rapidly have been those that helped individuals *know and develop their personalities and unique talents*. My "Finding Your Career Goals" workshops are always full because these seminars help people learn about themselves quickly as individuals.

Don't buck the tide. Invest in yourself and your continuing professional development. Your competition will. ➤

Be aware that the best and brightest employees leave when companies do not offer continuing and professional education.

Firms such as MCI, IBM, and AT&T are known for their recognition and investment in keeping their work force up-to-date. Today, the subjects most in demand in adult education are engineering and computer classes. It is expected that greater emphasis will be given to training in communication, self-esteem, conflict management, and interpersonal skills, particularly for managers.

Is your company willing to invest in you? If not, are you sure you're willing to continue investing in it? ➤

Acknowledge that there is no
perfect career.

Not too long ago, there were a lot of blacksmiths who didn't learn to work on cars and found fewer horses to shoe. There were featherbedding train workers who had ever-fewer trains to operate, coal miners who found the nation had turned to petroleum products for fuel, and factory workers who never thought they'd be replaced by automation.

Make change your ally. Understand that nothing can remain static. We must take care of our own career needs and speak up for ourselves. There is no longer a single-company career track. Know there are some things you cannot change and work you cannot achieve. Death will take people you love, and the way your personal and family life are ordered will not remain as they are today. Save your energy by channeling feelings of anger into productive self-analysis and action. While you may never find your *perfect* career, you can be sure that you can find your *right* career for now. ➤

Try the Baldwin

"Will-it-matter-in-two-weeks?"

test.

Somewhere back in the dark ages, someone, probably a mother, said, "If it's worth doing, it's worth doing well." There is a corollary. Lots of things *aren't* worth doing well and even more aren't worth doing at all!

Learn to prioritize and get results from only those efforts which are really important. Carry a little notebook around in your pocket for several days and jot down everything that *really* worries, frustrates, and makes you angry. This could be anything from the crowded traffic to and from work, your teenager's messy room or your boss's messy desk, the way a co-worker always clears his throat before he speaks, the boss's unreasonable demands, unwanted phone calls, or dirty dishes left in the sink. What you will find is that many of the things we worry about are little details not worth a minute of our concern.

Having gathered your list of things that bug you, apply the Will-it-matter-in-two-weeks? test. Starting with the easiest to let go, decide to eliminate that one item from being a bother in your life. Things like your son's strange haircut or messy room simply will not pass the test. Let go of them one after another. Then you begin to focus on the items on your list that really deserve your attention, such as making sure the computer program you write works, remembering your wife or husband's birthday, or selling up to your monthly quota. In other words, pick out the important items in your life and control only them while letting the others go.

Lastly, let go of the things you are unhappy about but cannot change like your complexion, the smog, your mother's depression, or your son's lack of mathematical ability. When in doubt, laugh. It's good for you! ➤

Become results-oriented; take
control of your fate.

There seem to be several ideals results-oriented people who deal well with change live by.

- They are risk takers who are challenged by new goals.
- They are committed to meeting those goals and getting results.
- They are self-directed and assertive about what they want to do, think, and feel.
- They have a sense of humor about themselves and their work.
- They are flexible in meeting and revising their goals.

- They plan and control their time.

In other words, these people on the leading edge of the Information Age will be in control of their own lives. They have many goals, so they are often successful (and they often fail, too). They are realistic and know they cannot possibly achieve all their goals, so they feel good about just learning from the struggles when a goal turns sour or fades from interest. They keep a sense of humor about themselves and what they do.

Actually, this is the way a good salesperson operates. To sell the product salespeople must approach not one or two but dozens of prospective customers, knowing they will probably fail with the majority, but every now and then making a sale and achieving a goal.

A perfectionist, on the other hand, calls all his unachieved goals "failures" and continues to seek the womb-to-tomb job, which is becoming a rare employment option today. Perfectionists are people often taken with themselves and their problems, with little interest in or understanding of others. They are usually humorless, unless they have found one of your mistakes, which gives them great glee. They want right or wrong answers and refuse to see the multiple options between. They often deny that they need to learn the self-knowledge and interpersonal skills that are so important in an age when machines continue to take over so many technical chores. (Afterall, it is not necessarily the best-qualified person who is hired, but the person who the interviewer likes the best!)

There are other ways in which you can begin to feel to control of your own life.

1. Daily set, change, and remind yourself of both your short- and long-range goals.

2. Make posters that remind you of your goal.

3. Take risks, but trust yourself.

4. Practice thinking about only the positives. Stop yourself every time a negative creeps into your mind.

5. Recall happy times and good memories, humorous and happy times. This will improve the way you feel.

6. Get started now to use the time today! ➤

Manage your time: this is the
key to productive job hunting.

One of the things I've noticed about my clients is that those who are the most self-directed also are often those who are least organized. They are results-oriented but sometimes lack the ability to stick to a goal or task long enough for completion because they are easily distracted. For these quick, physical, big-picture people who work best under the stress of deadline, here are some ideas.

1. Plan big-picture goals when away from the distractions of regular home and office environments.

2. Plan the week on Sunday night from notes and appointment schedules that have been gathered through the prior days, weeks, and months.

3. Each morning plan the day and prioritize agenda items. If something remains undone from the previous day, reschedule it if it's important. (Schedule in exercise and quiet time, too.)

4. As each item on the daily list is accomplished, enjoy the wonderful feeling that comes from being able to mark it off.

5. Mechanically stress yourself by setting a timer to ring. (After all, people who are very quick thinkers often work best under deadlines.) Usually just setting it for a fifteen-minute span is enough to get you started making the three or four calls or things on your desk you really seem to have a hard time doing—those things that keep getting moved from day to day on the to-do list.

6. Get away every now and then and plan to do nothing! ➤

Take command of your feelings
through self-talk.

Self-talk is language you use with yourself, and most of us are our own harshest critics. Negative self-talk is extremely powerful and will go a long way, especially in a job-hunting situation, toward defeating your efforts. You are selling self-confidence to a prospective employer. If you keep being overwhelmed, frustrated, angry, or resentful about what fate has dealt you, that will show in your ability to look like a good deal to any employer. This is why some people find jobs easily, while others repeatedly fail in interviews.

Since self-talk is so powerful, there are ways you can literally talk yourself into doing what you need to do.

You know how a results-oriented person would deal with an assignment with a very short time limit. First, he or she would organize the tasks into small "do"able tasks. Then he or she would say, "Let's see how much of this project I can finish," (*not* "I'd never be able to finish"). The positive talker says, often out loud, "Working hard makes my day go quickly," (*not* "I'd have to be a genius to finish all this stuff"). Positive says, "I'll gain a lot of confidence just by seeing how far I can get on this today." (Negative says, "I'll never be able to finish.") ➤

New Way #40

Always look for options with your present employer before making a change.

So many people get disgusted or distressed in their present job and fail to step back and understand what it is that makes them feel that way. So, first, if you do respect your company, see if you can find or create another job within the organization that fits your emotional or skill needs better. This job might be full or part time, depending on your desires.

One of the most usual reasons for wanting to change is a trying boss or co-worker. Are you happy doing what you do but simply in the wrong environment? Maybe this is the time to equip yourself with an employment proposal to give to a decision maker and invent yourself a new job. This is not a pie-in-the-sky idea; my clients do it every day. All you've got to do is figure out how you can make or save your company money. Then compose your wish list within that framework. ➤

When you see things beginning

to crumble in your job, don't

just stand by and wait to be

sacked.

When you find yourself forced to begin a job hunt, all your doubts about yourself and your abilities balloon to gigantic proportions. You may be angry and bitter. You may worry about fulfilling the dreams you had for yourself and your family. "Will I ever be able to afford to buy a home, send my children to college, take vacations, or start a family?" In addition, this is often a time of real difficulty for a marriage, a family, a friendship.

Job hunters often are paranoid and really weird!

Before you are forced into all the disagreeable changes of unemployment, you should *already* be hunting something new when you see your project nearing completion (this is the most frequent reason for lost jobs, by the way), your particular expertise is not as needed as before, or a buyout or merger is in the offing. It is vital that you plan and control any job change, making it your considered and self-directed decision—and not a forced decision that will instantly place you in the Slough of Despond! ➤

Manage employment change.

There is no good alternative! Concern about finding work should turn into the results-oriented challenge of doing the things every day that it will take to find it. If your emotions work as simply as mine do, you are lucky. I find that I can harbor only one strong emotion at a time. Enthusiasm about working on the details of a project totally blocks out any anxiety about not already having gained that result.

I learned this about myself in a rather interesting way. I had joined my sons and husband, who is quite a sportsman, in doing some mountain climbing in Colorado (rather than be left at home to worry). For months before we went, I ran daily to be in shape to accompany them. When we arrived, I did all the prerequisite mountain climbs to be able to climb The Mountain. During this physically demanding vacation, I quickly found that the emotional exhilaration overcame my fear! I could hang by a rope simply because I wanted to get where I was going, preferably as quickly as possible.

The corollary with job hunting is obvious. If you are busy doing the daily things that are described in the latter parts of this book, you will find that enthusiasm will overcome your impatience and fear. If you hide out at home, I *guarantee* you will become depressed. ➤

Acknowledge that unquestioned
loyalty is passé.

Remember, now *you* are in control of your own destiny. If you want flexibility, more money, or simply to stand out from the crowd, you must suggest ways your job could be handled more quickly and profitably, or how you could be trained so you can make or save more money for the company. This, of course, must meet the demands of both you and your employer.

Again, the womb-to-tomb job is gone. Unquestioned loyalty to a present position or employer is not terribly intelligent when you know that most companies are having to constantly revise and retool simply to stay in business. You will have many jobs, so those jobs might as well be on your terms. *In order to feel good about yourself, you must feel in control of your own fate.* ■

Chapter 5

Employment Trends

From Manhattan to San Francisco, Americans are undergoing dramatic changes in the patterns of their personal lives as well as the way they work. Census figures tell us too, that the white American male has been a minority in the work force since 1980. The Hispanic population is growing at four times that of the rest of the nation. Women are more apt to be employed than not.

What is in store for you and me, the workers who become unwanted because of changes in population, the economy, or new technology? ➤

Spot the trends that negatively
affect jobs.

We have noted some of the clues that tell us when jobs are likely to end. First, we now know that the number one reason for losing a job is simply that the project ends, an eventuality that you can plan for well in advance. The second reason for losing a job is a merger, buyout, or bankruptcy. Third is some sort of personal conflict or perceived inability to do the job.

Smart people are leaving behind the bitterness of lost employment knowing that it usually has nothing to do with them personally. Instead, they are *expecting* to revamp and enlarge their core of expertise, their skills, experiences, and training.

Also we know that the average age of college and technical school attendees is rising. Many people are electing (and others are being forced) to retool their minds for new careers. Some lucky ones are able to take advantage of job retraining offered by their employers. Keep an open eye! ➤

Know the trends likely to
affect your search.

1. *Self-directed, individualistic, time control.* As free time becomes a scarce commodity for working couples and single parents (who are the fastest-growing majority of households), time control becomes necessary. These workers want to tailor daily schedules to their individual needs rather than have schedules imposed on them by employers.

To no one's surprise, good pay is *not* the only thing that makes employees work. Employees are most interested in stimulating work and appreciation of good performance.

Americans want to piece together jobs, products, and services that best express them. The trend is away from social conformity and toward component lifestyles. Men are becoming more involved in shopping and families, while women increasingly work outside the home. A consumer may drive an expensive car, but we shop at discount stores.

2. *Most workers will have more than half a dozen jobs in their lifetimes.* We may even switch occupations two or three times, each time learning a different set of skills. The most important skills will be the ability to think and communicate—learning how to learn!

But many of us who are not as self-directed as the Information Age requires of us still seek what is no longer available—the womb-to-tomb job.

Thirty-five percent of the people in a University of Miami at Ohio survey believed working in a large organization offered the best opportunity for stable advancement. What those security-seekers don't realize is that fifty percent of the Fortune 500 companies existing in 1980 were *no longer in business* by 1989! All the ones that did remain had restructured and flattened their management pyramid.

3. *Elimination of the middle market* has a heavy bearing on the employment area. In 1989, my Hour Savers Career Services completed a four-and-a-half-month survey of forty top-level decision makers around the nation. Asked about their personnel practices and prejudices, I heard the following too often for it not be a trend: "There seems to be a marked divergence in quality between the professional workers and support employees—more than we've ever noticed before. Our professionals are the best we've ever had; our support people the worst."

4. *Use of temporaries, contract workers, and consultants much more than ever before.* The survey mentioned above also repeatedly mentioned this trend, which has been estimated by *The Wall Street Journal*, to be 25 percent of the new jobs, and growing.

The following are direct quotes, from decision makers from our survey, about their reasons for hiring temporary employees:

- "I don't have to provide any insurance, perks, or incentives."

- "It gives me a chance to look closely at prospective employees without the trouble and expenses of a full-blown hunt."

- "I can just let them go when no longer needed, and I don't have to go through the pain of laying them off"

■ "I can't find good full-time people for what I can pay."

5) *The healthiest generation in history is upon us* because of the rise in self-care. Smaller trends which tie to this are:

a) Self-imposed prohibition of alcohol and smoking (these now are no longer personal issues but social issues). Look for business ethics to be next!

b) The rise of group medical practices and the demise of the independent. The healthcare industry is in the midst of terrific change, and we will see vast changes because of runaway expenses.

c) By the year 2000, half of all medical care expenses will be spent for the care and treatment of Americans over age sixty-five. This is a profound change; it now accounts for one-third!

At the same time, the mental stress of dealing with uncertainty and lack of family support is exacting a rising toll in the workplace. Claims from workers citing anxiety reactions and other mental disorders rose sixfold between 1980 and 1987 in a western state with high employment. On a related note, it is estimated that well over 10 percent of our U.S. construction workers have problems with drug and alcohol abuse. Substance abuse causes up to 20 percent of workplace absenteeism and is often a factor in job related injuries.

6. *By the year 2000, middle age will be stylish,* and this has a terrific impact on employment. From 1989 to 2000, four million Americans will celebrate their thirty-fifth birthdays, joining the largest and most affluent segment of the population. So let's get to know these baby boomers with whom we are already dealing the majority

of the time. They grew up being told they could have it all, *now*, and at work they will continue to make demands. These demands include

a. Benefits, free time, pleasant surroundings, and a say in decisions

b. More initiative and less mobility because of working spouses

If *you* are Boomer, it might interest you to know

a. You will probably be a homeowner, perhaps with help from inheritances (since Boomers' parents, now over sixty-five, represent only 20 percent of U.S. households, but have one trillion dollars in personal financial assets—about 40 percent of the U.S. total).

b. You have a resurrected (from casual) sense of dress-for-success stylishness.

c. You probably like individual sports, active travel.

d. You probably eat sophisticated, experimental, varied, convenient, ethnic, fresh, and healthful food. You'll see restaurants, especially fast-food places, shift their focus to foods more suitable to your tastes.

e. Your children, the Echo Boom, the oldest of whom are fourteen years old in 1991, are a much larger group than the prior Baby Bust generation. You will see growth in needs for adolescent groups, runaway shelters, etc. You are likely already to be swamped with child-care needs.

7. *A resurgence in family-oriented values* is evident despite delayed marriages, delayed childbearing, and a growth of women in the workforce.

Since working women still bear most the homemaking and child-rearing responsibilities in two-income households, one of the challenges for Boomers is to find ways to help balance the competing demands of work and home.

These demands will be met by

a. Day-care plans and after-school pick-up programs, as well as parental leave

b. Flexible benefit (cafeteria) programs

c. Flexible working hours

Working fathers will demand more time to be with their children, although employers today don't make it easy for them to do so. (I know of an attorney who was let go because he was trying to fairly share the family demands— the children's carpools, etc.—with his working wife.)

8. *Tomorrow's workers will be increasingly female, minority, and older.* Finding enough workers will be a growing problem. A survey of nearly 14,000 businesses indicated that thirty percent plan to increase staffs, and only six percent anticipate cutbacks. About sixty-one percent expect their employment numbers to remain stable (but maybe not with the same employees).

More than half of women employees will have babies while they are employed.

Companies will begin to scramble to fill vacancies with available workers. The birth rate is not high enough to replace workers after they leave the workforce. The labor market is expected to grow less than two percent in the next few years, half of the rate of 1970s. Among the reasons is that one-third of the jobless are poor work prospects (people who are students, ill, institutionalized, on drugs, too illiterate to meet the demands of today's very technical work, or who have unsuccessfully looked for employment for more than a year).

Employers will turn to good sources of workers: the fourteen million women who stay home to take care of children and the three million early retirees. You will see firms lure workers from other companies with higher pay, putting more upward pressure on wages and allowing the job hunter more opportunity!

Recruiting workers will cost more. So will training workers in basic and job-related skills.

The trend toward hiring older workers is already appearing at the very top and bottom of the wage scale. Thousands of people who have been pushed out of the job market because they had reached the magic (or tragic) age of fifty-five have now become our newest group of entrepreneurs and consultants. Learning to market their companies and themselves, these older—but certainly not elderly—Americans are determined to stay employed. America in the Information Age cannot afford to permanently retire the brains packed with the most information, for information (or synthesized knowledge) is what *we* have to sell to the world! ➤

Plan your career advancement around corporate-sponsored training, the most rapidly growing segment of education.

As we have noted, the most humane and forward-thinking companies are retraining employees to retain and get a good return on their human investments. If you find such a company, target it! If you can instigate for change in this direction in your own current company, do so! ➤

Be acutely aware of those companies and employers that are willing to hire workers from other industries.

Not every company is willing to take on an outsider. Most service areas, however, are more flexible. These more open-minded managers are usually in financial services, data processing, health-care industries, and employee training. Usually, the smaller and less bureaucratic the organization, the more open-minded management is likely to be. ➤

Understand where the coming
jobs will be.

Eighty-five percent of the new work force will be in the four Information Age areas: high tech, environmental organizations, health-care industries, and the elder market, which serves older consumers. (Those elders will be busy entrepreneurs—consultants, financial managers, and community service workers. This is one population segment from which employers can tap experienced workers who don't usually need nor necessarily want enormous salaries.) ➤

Consider the environmental field if you're seeking employment in an area resistant to economic downturns.

Waste water management, waste disposal management, and air/ground/water pollution fields have shown great buoyancy to the economic uncertainties of today. These companies (besides needing chemists, engineers, and other technical people) must market and sell their services or product, as well as administer and financially oversee their companies. (Add to the environmental field the traditionally solid jobs in insurance sales and undertaking.) ➤

Consider every option when looking for work.

At the outset, many of my clients either have their heart set on working at a particular job for a particular company (usually for all the wrong reasons), or have no idea what job they want at all. Knowing yourself and your area of expertise is the first step. Then target at least two, hopefully three, possible areas in which your interests, education, and experience would be assets. Even consider the military services or moving to another area, if necessary.

Look first inside the company in which you are presently employed unless you're *absolutely* leaving *no matter what!* Then concurrently make contacts in two or three areas, so if one isn't hiring perhaps another will be on the upswing.

Also think about returning for more training. (If you're not computer literate, for instance, you can find yourself either quickly having to pay to train yourself or find yourself out of consideration for a job you know you can do.) ➤

Dare to intern.

I have friends who seriously contemplated investing in their own business some day; while the wife worked at her regular job, the husband approached a company and offered his work on an internship basis for two weeks to gain relevant experience. He turned out to be such a good contributor to the company coffers that he was hired full time!

Others have used the same ploy intentionally to win a job. As an employer, it's hard to resist a person who's so enthusiastic that he or she is willing to work for next to nothing. Consider this idea as a sort of an internship for older workers, not just students. ➤

Consider working at home

instead of the office.

Home work is growing, organized around tasks accomplished rather than hours spent in an office or plant. It is an excellent way to avoid traffic, maintain a lower overhead, and win the kind of flexibility most of us would kill for. I know many managers who spend a day or so a week working at home away from distractions. Remember, it's often to the employer's benefit as well as yours to make such an arrangement! ➤

Target today's job growth areas.

A. The Sunbelt states will capture the bulk of new jobs. The most promising jobs today are

B. ■ High tech. Computer maintenance, network specialists, telecommunications, robotics, artificial intelligence, computer graphics, data bank management.

■ People caring for people. Doctors, nursing, nutrition, elder care, child care, and home health care.

■ Environmentally related jobs, such as waste-water specialists. Cleaning up the environment is *big* business.

■ Stress relievers, such as therapists and counselors of all kinds.

■ Security and security systems to serve an increasingly crowded society.

■ Remedial education; it is expected that 65 percent of all U.S. corporations will have remedial education programming for employees by the year 2000.

■ Chefs and food preparers for restaurants because working mothers don't have as much time to cook.

■ Genetic and biomedical engineering.

C. Also travel-related jobs, legal assistance (paralegals), laser/fiber optics, corporate TV, physical therapy, electrical/civil engineering, marine ecology, and appliance and auto repair.

Remember, if your job can help others save time, it will probably thrive. ■

Chapter 6

Know Yourself and What You Want

When it comes to finding career direction, the person we have least control of is ourselves. So: how do we assess our own talents, skills, and experience so we can point ourselves in a way which will make us both happy and productive? ➤

Discover how to find out what you want to be when you grow up.

The first rule for finding a fulfilling position is having goals. You simply must know what you want and have that core of knowledge which makes you valuable to a prospective employer (and also different from the competition). Why should an employer hire you otherwise?

As a full-time returnee to the work force when our children were in their teens, I decided that I would (after relocating because of my husband's career) find or make a job for myself that would be uniquely tailored to my gifts and experience. In short, I would find work that made me happy.

So this is what I did.

1. I listed every project carried out and the duties of every job ever held or any I ever wanted to do. This task took about three weeks because these thoughts usually only came to me right before I went to sleep or while I was driving on the freeway! I included every position held (which were many) and added all the organizational, college, and church leadership positions in which I had been involved. Next I skimmed the want ads to see if anything there sounded interesting. (Unrestricted dreaming and free-flowing thought is a plus at this stage.)

2. Then I drew a line through everything I would *never* do again (short of starvation); then another line through everything that wouldn't provide a living wage.

3. Next, I put check marks by those that I really enjoyed doing.

(4.) I analyzed all those remaining to discover what skills and abilities these jobs required. I listed them.

Your list might look something like this:

Experience	Skills
Inventory control	math/sequential thinking
x computer operation	math/typing
customer service	communication
x record keeping	organize paperwork
supervise warehouse staff	leadership/communication
sell "add ons" to service	communication
x repair machinery	mechanical
wait on drop-in customers	communication
x order and stock parts	detail/coordination
x pack and order shipments	detail/coordination

The x's fall next to items that indicate that this person prefers dealing with things rather than people. He could market to a prospective employer his mechanical, math detail, organization, and coordination skills. The kind of jobs he does best then become very obvious.

Using this common-sense and street smart approach, the list will quickly point you on the way. If you have difficulties, ask a friend or trusted relative to help you see this list objectively. ➤

See if these self-evaluation
suggestions help you.

- Are you a mover and shaker who likes to run the show? Do you always end up with major responsibility? (This usually illustrates leadership ability, verbal quickness, results orientation, ability to work under deadlines.)

- Do you like delegating or do you tend to take tasks back to do them right? (Persuaders like delegating. People who must totally control make poor supervisors and would be better off working with things rather than people.)

- On what do you repeatedly receive compliments? What do your mother, wife, or husband tell you that you do easily and well? (Those around you often are very perceptive, if you'll only listen and not succumb to the "Prophet in Your Own Land" Syndrome.)

- Do your like to work alone with things or numbers, or do your prefer a job making things happen through people? (If you like people and can stand duties such as firing and reprimanding, you should consider supervisory management. If you prefer things or numbers, steer clear of supervision of others.)

- Do you like jobs that offer you a chance to have a scheduled routine and to be methodical, or are you at your best when able to move about, be physically flexible, and use your many ideas? ("Things" people are happier with routine and threatened by change.

"People" people need both physical and intellectual flexibility and usually are easily bored and seek variety.)

- Are you better when you work under an organizational framework that structures your time, or are you so self-motivated that working under strong supervision is constantly irritating to your results orientation? (Quick thinkers often need that framework to control their time; strong achievers are usually self-motivated and resent anyone controlling their already well-organized time.)

Answers to questions like these should quickly tell you

- Whether you are self-motivated and could easily take responsibility for your own work

- Whether you always end up being the leader or whether you want exact direction on how a task should be done

- Whether you need a quiet job in a large company that offers you employment security. (Job security is becoming more and more elusive. Don't count on it if you can help it.)

Now you can probably also pick out the skills you really enjoy, such as working with machines, organizing, writing, dealing with people, coordinating projects, research, computer programming. Ask your best friend or relative to finish this sentence for you. "Bob/Jane has always been good at." This exercise will help you see your traits as others see you. Next step: seeking jobs in which a majority of your strengths will be used. ➤

Check out these final notes on career goals.

National surveys usually cite these six reasons, in descending order of importance, as the most common factors in a decision to change jobs.

1. Personality conflict

2. Want more/less responsibility

3. Seek more challenge

4. Need more money

5. Feel need of compatible environment

6. Want more status or title

7. Seek advancement

If you could order your life as you wanted from the above list, which would be your number one? two? three? Rank the whole list (and feel free to add your own reasons), and you'll have some idea of the kind of environment that would make you happiest.
➤

Consider what most people want

from their jobs.

√ 1. Challenge and change

2. Security

3. Compatible team members

√ 4. Opportunity

√ 5. Responsibility

√ 6. Money

7. Company car

8. Living where you want

√ 9. Status

10. Insurance coverage

√ 11. Industry growth

√ 12. Personal advancement

13. Opportunity for spouse's career

Of these, which are most important to you? ➤

Learn to measure career
decisions by your goals.

When you chart your job hunting plan, write your resume, or attend an interview, you will be wise to measure whatever detail you are considering by asking yourself, "Is it relevant to my goal?" To use this yardstick you must know what your goals are. Without goals, efforts usually result in lack of momentum and a loss of persistence, hereinafter called *glue*.

 What, first of all, are your ultimate goals? What do you want to be when you have reached the top of your particular totem pole? Be flexible, since we are in the midst of a rapidly changing economic era; circumstances, values, and motivations will be subject to change as time passes. These days you can almost count on having to revise today's goal within less than five years. However, you do need an overall plan for your work life, short-term objectives within that plan, and some sort of very flexible timetable for getting there. Knowing where you want to go—having direction—makes all the difference in how you act. ➤

Don't fall in love with the romance of what you think a job or career is going to be.

Inform yourself by talking with several people in the field beforehand. For instance, know that working in the travel field is not all free tickets and foreign travel. It is often low pay and bad hours. Don't become a lawyer just because they make a lot of money. Attorneys also perform a lot of tedious tasks and find themselves in unfriendly, adversarial positions. In fact, today more than 30 percent of all lawyers would leave the field if they had known what it was really going to be like! ➤

New Way #60

**Don't give in to peer pressure;
the job you prefer may not be
the one that is in style with
your acquaintances.**

Your real friends will want you to be employed in a field that *you* enjoy, even if that means taking a lesser salary or not having a swanky office. Other "friends" will steer you in a different direction. Remember: if everyone were enjoying the great salaries and business perks you hear about at happy hours, business would be broke. *People lie.* Do what fits your gifts and interests. ➤

New Way #61

**Grasp this straw if you still
can't discover your goals.**

If you still find yourself totally lost at sea concerning your goals, try the exercises in Barbara Sher's book *Wishcraft*. She found her way to career success after being left with three children to support in an expensive city (New York), armed only with a "dinosaur" degree and no work experience. ➤

Ask yourself if it all adds up.

Analyze your interests (which change) by the criteria of skills and aptitudes.

For instance, let's see if my work as job hunt counselor, resume and business writer, lecturer and corporate trainer fulfills my skills, aptitudes, and emotional needs. Well, first of all, the following are my easily spotted attributes:

- *Efficiency.* Use time well and am organized.

- *Results oriented.* Quick to finish material, flexible about editing my words or adapting a speech (because all I want for my clients are results).

- *People skills.* Work daily with both private and corporate clients.

- *Self-motivated.* Willing to take the risk of heading my own business so I can control who I work with, what I do.

- *Eager for recognition* gained through radio, TV, speeches, and seminar appearances, quotes in media, books. ➤

Weigh your goal for realism.

Will you have to go back to college or take other training classes, or overcome many difficulties along the way? Is that worth it to you? If you think not, rethink the goal. Do you think you could become the best of whatever you want to do, whether it be welder, president, accountant, bookkeeper, computer analyst, salesperson, or executive recruiter? ■

Chapter 7

Enlarge Your Core of Expertise

My client Cathy sat next to me in tears, "Why can't I just go to a personnel agency and let them find me a job?"

Cathy had, as have most of us, been brought up with a womb-to-tomb job mentality. Also, she suffered from one of the most common of all job hunt diseases: wanting somebody *else* to take this pain away. Cathy had been in school seemingly forever, from kindergarten through high school, four years of college, and then studied in Europe. She had been on an escalator that always moved toward an assumed known: make good grades and get a degree and everything will be okay. A job and/or marriage will automatically follow.

Now her parents, who had always helped Cathy through little difficulties, had run out of both money (and patience) as she reached her mid-twenties. And partly because things had come easily as long as she did the right things, Cathy was now deathly afraid of facing the competition out there in the real world, because that world was *not* the one for which her education or her family had prepared her!

How to respond to this dilemma? ➤

Understand what core of

expertise means.

1. Aptitudes (spatial, number memory, logic, innate emotional steadiness, natural organization ability). Today most people have been exposed to some sort of academic career testing that helped them discover these basic aptitudes. I have found, however, that many people do not attempt to incorporate these tests into their search for career happiness. If you don't, that testing becomes a pointless exercise and a waste of everyone's time!

2. Learned technical skills (typing, photography).

3. Experience in a definite area (cost accounting, production management, editing, counseling, fast-food management, contract negotiating, plumbing, elementary teaching).

(If you have not discovered your core, please turn back to chapter 6 and try some of the tricks for quick career self-analysis outlined there.) ➤

Direct your own core of

expertise.

In the midst of this monumental change, what is the individual to do? Become self-directed, that's what! Become that person who is most valuable to this coming information society; one who has a core of expert knowledge and personality assets that they can sell, not just in one direction but very flexibly in several. Know what your assets are and how that expertise translates into specific kinds of jobs.

Let me illustrate by going back to our story. I'm happy to report that Cathy on another day was able to begin to be a realist about her job hunt and sit with me quietly and seriously to discover her core, then plan her strategies. Cathy will probably never *like* searching for work, but at least she learned what she has to market—her core of expertise. Her core turned out to be organization, spatial aptitude, interior design experience, clerical skills, and good education. We suggested she use this initially as an interior design assistant, design researcher and analyst, and/or design project coordinator.

Cathy has learned about herself, as well as the techniques for making the job hunt less painful because the chances are she— and you as well—will have to hunt for jobs several times in a lifetime. And she also has found the value of a sense of humor as well as the strength that is gained only through personal struggle and a *realistic* knowledge of herself and what she is facing. ➤

Note this second example of
having a core of expertise.

Mike was a geologist. He worked for fifteen years for a major oil company but lost his job when U.S. oil exploration was curtailed, his company declined and was sold. Finding another U.S. job when many petroleum geologists were unemployed would have been difficult if not impossible for Mike, whose interpersonal skills were lacking. Mike was a good geologist who loved his work and was very technically inclined.

These are the three routes we worked out for Mike to continue to use his technical core:

1. International oil exploration work

2. Returning to a university for some ground water geology coursework and starting in that strong environmental field

3. Corporate consulting until other jobs could be secured

Mike is now doing international work, traveling extensively, and thoroughly enjoying it. But he always knows he can go back to the university and update his water knowledge in the future if need be. And he's saving appropriately in case that becomes necessary. ➤

Take time to match talents in your core to your employer's needs.

Paul was a client who had a manner that was quick, impatient, and self-assured. Every time I broached a new subject, he already knew more than I did; my three decades of hard-won experience in the area were quickly brushed aside. Paul bombed in interview after interview; his self-involved cockiness quickly eliminated him. Another problem was his unrealistic time schedule for finding work (three months for an entry-level position is the national average); in addition, his egotistical attitude led him to begin his career search without doing his homework. He needed to understand what the *employer* needed and match that with his talents. (A little more tact was in order, as well.) ➤

Understand that military
retirees have to learn to sell
their core, too.

Edward, a man in his forties who had retired as an officer from the military, was learning for the first time how to look for employment. His background had taught him to do as he was told in an orderly manner. The more flexible and creative people skills he was going to need to find employment in civilian life were foreign and, worse, not *right* (a word frequently used by scared perfectionists). He was, in short, very uncomfortable with American business and how it really operates today.

Hence, Edward, like a great many military retirees, found the job hunt an emotional roller coaster; he made three (the usual average) job changes before being able to settle into something as permanent as anything can be these days. By that time, however, *he'd honed his sales skills.* Today Edward is president of a corporation. And his company is successful mainly because of Edward's ability to use not only his strong leadership background, but also his newly identified and educated core to make profitable contacts through people.

(All of these examples are typical of the many ways we react to the ever-increasing necessity for job change and search. Paul found it difficult to stop long enough to arm himself with the information about himself and the company that would make him look more intelligent. Cathy and Edward had trouble at first leaving home to use the information with people.) ■

Chapter 8

Widen Your Options by Finding Words to Sell Yourself

One of the initial questions you'll hear from a prospective employer will be, "What do you want to do?"

How will you answer? ➤

Be ready to explain what you want to do.

If "What do you want to do?" is a question you cannot answer, you are not yet organized enough to look your professional best as you enter today's job market.

By now you should have uncovered your flexible goal or goals—the core career or jobs that interest you most. You realize and have listed the skills required by that job. Now, you will begin to uncover your value to any organization. ➤

Be able to discuss articulately
the technical side of your work.

Count on much of your interview time being taken up with inquiries about the tasks involved in your current or most recent work.

Should you feel uncomfortable and tongue-tied when attempting to talk about your work in specific terms, now is the time to start explaining to family, friends and your dog Spot exactly what you do. Nothing helps as much as having to talk about it frequently. Tape explanations when you find yourself stumbling, so you can clean up your sentences and smooth out your answers. ➤

Learn to transfer your skills into the language used to market yourself.

Learn to transfer your skills into words you can use to quickly describe yourself on the telephone and in interviews later on.

When working with a client, I always tape two or three assertive replies to "What do you want?" The replies often sound something like this: "I have three areas in which I am competent: technical computer system liaison, user training, and administrative customer support."

Now, using your written list of skills, prepare a concrete illustration for each, because people remember specific incidents rather than vague generalities. Here are some examples:

- Interacting with people is one of my strongest assets. When I was with ACE I was the person with a knack for calming difficult customers on the telephone, and I was cited for saving a $200,000 account!

- I've an eye for analytical detail. I received an award for saving my company $500 per month on telephone charges, just by taking the initiative to pick up billing mistakes.

- In my last position in sales support, there was friction between the technical staff and the sales force. I served as a liaison—as a sort of a go-between who translated the needs of one group to the other in order to accomplish what the company had promised its customers. ➤

Use your skills list to boost your self-confidence.

When your self-confidence tends to waver, go over your skills list again. Simply noting these strengths can be a real ego booster.
➤

Quickly list your very few weaknesses, so you can avoid them.

For heaven's sake, don't dwell on them and batter yourself, as a fearful perfectionist would do!

As an example, I know that under time pressures I become a doer rather than a delegator, and not only tend to take back delegated work and to do it right, but also communicate very ineffectively. As a result, I watch out for these loner tendencies. At the same time, I avoid putting myself in positions where I have to constantly delegate.

Under deadlines, many of us turn into almost another person. The quick thinker is usually better under a definite deadline because that focuses his quick (and often erratic) thinking. Without the constraints of time, he interrupts himself (or goes down the hall and forgets why he left his cubicle). ➤

Review your skills list to pinpoint the things you like to do.

Go back to your list and check the things that made you love going to work.

Perhaps you loved your job because

- Of the role you played

- Your skills and interests were well matched to your area of expertise

- You were able to contribute

- You played a role that made you look good. ➤

Uncover what you have that makes you "different in a nice way."

This is a direct quote from my mother that I heard for eighteen years at least three times weekly.

Now, what is unique about you? What is the strongest attribute that runs through all of this probing of interests and self? This is what you highlight on your resume, in conversations, and interviews.

We listed such assets for a client who is now a company president but had spent his earlier years in the military: leadership, generation of bottom-line ideas, ability to motivate others to rise above their own expectations, and international contacts. You can see how perfect he was to lead a company into business overseas, and he has done very well using these very assets to expand his organization. ➤

5) Technical expertise in EE of highest caliber combined with MBA of highest caliber which focuses towards business orientation

Copy the following real example of turning your assets into a way to call prospective employers on the telephone.

Hello, my name is Mary Anne Black. John Brown told me to call you. I'm thinking of making a career change. I have a background in customer service, sales, inventory or document control, and shipping/receiving areas. I'm familiar with Apple computers. I attended Texas Christian University and Eastfield College. Do you have a couple of minutes to give me some advice? I am not asking you for a job. Because of my heavy work and college schedule, I have not had the time until now to ask questions of people who would be knowledgeable about the Portland job market. I need someone to help me find some direction. Career testing recently said that my personal traits were innovative problem solving, self-reliance, persistence, and having a direct and honest personality. I have raised a son and daughter alone, leading my daughter through a relearning process to complete recovery from a childhood stroke. I've worked hard and flexibly to do whatever needed to be done. I never missed work because of illness and have never been late. Past employers have called me mature and stable, results oriented, one who loves a challenge, and one who wears well with co-workers.

Questions you would then ask could include:

1. Can you give me some idea of the market there is for my specialty in the Portland area?

2. Do you know where someone with my experience should be applying?

3. Can you describe the person you have supervised in that position who you thought was the best you ever had? What was their personality like and what technical expertise did they possess?

4. Do you know any managers to whom I could talk directly?

5. May I use your name when calling them? ■

Chapter 9

Employment Proposals: The New Resume

Since an ever smaller minority of us work in large companies such as IBM, it's up to each of us to suggest to our prospective or present employer work and training arrangements that satisfy us *and* help the corporation make or save money! ➤

Know when to use an employment
proposal.

An employment proposal can be used after you have been interviewed to gain a larger salary, or to counter an initial salary offer and edge out your competition. The main criteria for writing a proposal, though, is knowledge of the job or company in order to fill the boss's or organization's needs.

Repeatedly, I've had clients complain about their jobs, only to find that they've never approached their own or prospective employers with new suggestions or, if they have, were afraid of threatening an insecure boss.

Today, innovative companies are taking all kinds of suggestions from their employees as well as those interested in working for the organization. Besides being a way to design yourself a job, sometimes suggestions include changes like four-day work weeks, job sharing, daily and weekly flextime, and time off for formal education. Xerox even gives paid leave for community service.

It is often to the company's benefit to have a very flexible and creative work force. Remember, part-time, project, consulting, and contract positions now account for over a quarter of the new jobs, and that piece of the pie is growing rapidly! ➤

Consider writing an employment proposal in place of a resume.

This kind of proposal outlines what you can do to make or save money for the company (and make your boss look good at the same time). Thus having established yourself as a results-oriented bottom-liner with the boss, you have the clout to be assertive enough to ask for some things for yourself. If the company is totally unresponsive, then you can always look elsewhere, because *you and you only* are in control of your career and life. A proposal is best used when you

- Are already employed by the company doing contract, consulting, or lower-level work and you'd like to better yourself within the corporation

- Know a great deal about the company, this particular position, and what you could bring to it

- Have been tentatively offered the job, but their pay or duties are below your expectations

- Are in competition for the new job and want to bolster your employment chances

This employment proposal can be written in letter form if you have a friend known to the decision maker; use his or her name for a hook in the first paragraph to quickly grab the reader's attention. But the employment proposal will be more effective if you either set up an appointment to hand deliver the proposal or have someone close to the decision maker do so.

Typically, the proposal sets out to tell the decision maker, in quick one- or two-page bullet form, how much money, time, or hours they could save or earn by hiring you! Following are some examples of slightly altered real proposals. ➤

Scan this proposal—it was used

---

to gain a larger salary after

---

the initial sales job offer had

---

been made.

James J. Polk—Employment Proposal

As the person that our mutual friend, John Brown, sees as one who does what needs to be done, proven initiative is one of the strongest assets I can bring to ABC. Also, both executives and co-workers have remarked on my can-do attitude and ability to be a team player. I do more than simply sell a product.

Because of my experience, I can be immediately valuable to your bottom line, and I would expect any compensation offer to reflect the value of that experience.

These are some of the things I've done to enhance revenues in the past:

- Established a prestigious brand account and increased those sales alone from $5,000 in 1986 to $25,000 in 1989, in a sparsely populated area of the West

- Organized and conducted direct mail, telemarketing, personal contact, and speaking events to civic groups

- Served as part of the original team that set up a New York showroom, helping meet the annual goal within the first seven days

- Consulted with newly established accounts for initial merchandising and product display

- Prepared display and merchandising for other New York showrooms earlier in my career

- Used broad personal and social contacts for sales leads

- Created and managed a successful retail gift business
➤

Use this employment proposal to
put employer doubts to rest.

A client wrote this as a follow-up to a two-page proposal to counter doubts about his ability to negotiate. He was already temporarily employed in a clerical job inside the corporation.

Addendum to Employment Proposal
John J. Brown

In further contemplation of how I can be most valuable to ABC, these are my thoughts following recent conversations.

Since the firm operates under several different names, applying economies of scale to purchasing, personnel, administrative, accounting, and risk management functions could save thousands annually. These are all areas in which I have definite experience and the proven ability to negotiate both savings and better service, as shown by the following:

- Negotiated national and international freight service contracts for shipment of both parts and finished products.

- Oversaw adherence to quality specifications on bids to national and international customers, including governments.

- Negotiated all types of insurance, including vehicle, product liability, health, life, fire/theft, and business loss. This function included choice of carriers and the oversight/enforcement of safety requirements as outlined by insurance companies and governmental agencies.

- Provided necessary legal documentation and follow-up for bad debt lawsuits.

- Developed and enforced credit policy with new and existing customers (including international), despite initial resistance to these new policies. These policies allowed more efficient and realistic cash budgeting. Obviously, I am suited to work with vendors in a similar, diplomatic manner.

As a self-starter in every position I've held, initiative is one of the strongest assets I can bring to ABC. Additionally, supervisors and peers have always commented on my good attitude and ability to work as part of the team. ➤

Try this employment proposal to increase your chances of getting the job after interviewing.

Employment Proposal for XYZ Corporation
Harvey Smith

XYZ is an expanding business with plans to become one of the country's top five dealers by the end of the decade. To meet this challenge, XYZ needs a solid and innovative support staff. Presently, the business office needs direction and organization to support this expanding enterprise. My experience can provide that direction and organization.

Accounting Changeover and Operation Experience

- Oversaw implementation of on-line accounting systems for two prior employers. Was solely responsible for all facets of systems from order entry to preparation of monthly/annual financials. Can quickly analyze and learn accounting software so that new system can be up and running in a few months.

- Implemented controls/policies/procedures for entire corporate structure, including treatment of cash purchase/sales, revision of order entry process and more rapid product delivery. Efficiency and profitability were both improved.

- Solved problems and acted as liaison with vendors and staff on a daily basis. Through my interpersonal skills, I was able to keep materials flowing to plant even under difficult cash-flow situations.

- Acted as a quick and reliable source of financial/legal/operational information as requested by department. Also advised staff on international cash management, product export, customs and contract negotiation.

- Efficiently handled increased operational responsibilities as track record warranted. Have twice begun as a staff accountant and risen to lead the department and to act as a special aide to executive management. Effective hands-on management background; fair and equitable with staff.

- Big-picture thinker able to delegate. Have broad experience in running a company from financial to operational management.

- Accustomed to giving presentations to corporate heads and boards. Flexible, can be polished or casual as environment dictates. ➤

Try this employment proposal to gain a job where you have been working contract and want to stay.

J.R.B. — Employment Proposal

Turner Institute plans to expand their offices to other sections of the United States. Because of this expansion, the need for experienced and solid regional managers is already being discussed with the corporate staff. My background can help you quickly to gain the kind of results that Turner wants.

- **Coordinated educational programming** for leadership institutes, motivational training, and individual chapter leadership.

- **Generated record number of membership sales** at trade shows, and had highest number of new member and renewal sales.

- **Supervised staff of 14.** Hired, dismissed, trained, scheduled, supervised and reviewed.

- **Financial experience.** Began career in accounting and worked in most financial positions with three companies. Oversaw all accounting functions and staff.

As you have seen from my contract work here at Turner, I am the kind of loyal and productive team member that you can count on for results. Could we discuss a mutually satisfactory permanent relationship? ➤

Combine an employment proposal

---

with a personal thank-you note

---

when you know a hiring decision

---

will be made quickly and you

---

have competition.

To Mr. Joseph Abelson
Terri Howell—Employment Proposal—Trainer
Telefono is an expanding telecommunications telemarketing service with plans to quickly integrate the two parent companies.

To meet this challenge, Telefono needs a solid and innovative staff to train and support this exciting enterprise. My experience and work style can help your team provide that direction and organization.

- **12 years teaching and training experience** includes curriculum development, instruction and supervision of teachers, as well as strong communication skills, patience, and sensitivity

- **Telemarketing background** with a marketing research firm

- **Business and sales support experience** with a major manufacturer

- **Customer and community liaison experience** with two school districts and a major retailing chain

- **B.S., Education, 1977,** from East Missouri State.

As an enthusiastic employee in every position I've held, organized professionalism is one of the strongest assets I can bring to Telefono. Additionally, past peers and supervisors have always commented on my good attitude and ability to work as part of the team.

Mr. Abelson, what more can I do to qualify for this job?

(My client than added a short, handwritten thank-you note to the bottom of this proposal.) ∎

Chapter 10

Write a New-Style Resume (And, If Needed, a Cover Letter)

First of all, let's relegate the resume to its real importance. You cannot place a piece of paper between you and a potential employer and hope to get a job, because ultimately everything happens through people. I know it seems so much easier to mail something, but in the long run it really is *not* the easy way because it is supremely unproductive. Not only that, but getting no feedback after mailing all those resumes and answering all those ads will lower your self-confidence—and confidence (not cockiness) is one of the major attributes you are selling to a prospective employer. ➤

Understand why you write a
resume in the first place.

Resumes, at their best, help you organize your work life so you can talk about it. They act more as verification of your professionalism than a tool for obtaining a job. In fact, they are most often used as a way to screen you out! Whenever you mail a resume, the Las Vegas odds are against you. Employers like to make *their* task of screening applicants simpler, hence the popularity of resumes as a requirement for employment. ➤

Forget traditional job-seeking techniques.

These include private and public employment agencies, school placement offices, newspaper advertisements, and job lists. These methods actually work for a very small percentage of us. It is estimated that eighty percent of all vacancies are not available through traditional channels, which means approximately four out of five jobs are filled by word of mouth (through people, in other words).

So, the idea that to land a job you mail out resumes—and more resumes and more resumes—is obviously incorrect. If you use all your time and effort to prepare the right resume to match each job, then the really important items like making contacts with friends and acquaintances, seeking job leads, preparing for interviews, and keeping up your morale become secondary.

Actually, a trade magazine recently conducted an interesting survey on this score. This study found companies received 245 resumes before they sent out a single interview invitation. Fifty percent of those invitations were ignored (probably because the applicant who sent the resume had since found a job through crazy Uncle Harold).

Additionally, only one real interview took place for each 490 resumes received. Finally, three actual interviews took place for every job offer made, which means 1,470 (three times 490) resumes had to be received for every job actually secured! ➤

Learn to sidestep Personnel or

Human Resources Departments.

It is not uncommon for a person to be rejected through their resume or interview with Personnel, then to later find a door open to the decision maker and be hired.

Remember, the resume reader is trying to figure out what kind of employee you'll be by glancing at your past experiences. If you have many jobs, the reader screens you out because you look unstable, whether you are or not. I have had clients who have had the bad luck to work for three consecutive companies that have gone out of business through no fault of their own.

Judging people's value by their length of service in one job is passe today. But, most personnel departments are still frozen in such thinking and can be counted on to judge you heavily by dates and longevity. Avoid them! ➤

Quit searching for the perfect resume.

There *is* no perfect resume. Each reader (who gives you only an instant of attention) brings his own prejudices and viewpoint to what is written. In short, if that piece of paper does not make you look as if you fit the recipe that Personnel/Human Resources has been given, you are screened out.

So why write a resume at all? Because it orders your thinking and helps you sell yourself more effectively. And, well done, it can be that verification of your professionalism, as much a part of your image as the good-looking suit, polished shoes, quiet hair, and portfolio. ➤

Spot the differences between traditional and creative resumes.

And, please, leave the traditional, and most widely used Harvard (or chronological) resume style in the Yard! That's the resume an English teacher probably taught you to write in school. You can usually identify it because the dates are lined up on the left side of the page and there is a paragraph after each date. The Harvard style sells dates, but hopefully you have managed to do more than exist! Practically speaking, the chronological resume is one of the very poorest resume styles. ➤

Discern the importance of the far left side of the resume page.

Use some street smarts and use that precious left side of the page (since we read from left to right in English) for really important things (like hard verbs that denote action, recognizable company names, or job titles that show your progression and advancement through the ranks). ➤

Accept that a resume is a foot in the door.

It is neither your life history nor your obituary. Decision makers want to know what you can do to make or save money for them. The simplest way to illustrate this is to include hooks: specific, concrete accomplishments highlighted so that the eyes are immediately drawn to them. Hooks make you memorable, for we recall pictures of specifics, not vague job descriptions. Grab the reader's eyes—quickly—to make yourself stand out from the crowd. ➤

Compose a different-in-a-nice-way resume,

Use the ideas on the following pages as a quick and easy-to-follow handbook to writing an eye-catching and effective resume. ➤

Realize why resumes should be brief.

Resumes are usually one or two pages; it's presumptuous to think anyone but your mother cares to read more than that. And, should you be seeking a sales job, try your hardest to keep it to one page. Why? Because the typical salesperson is quick to think and articulate; rarely does that kind of person possess the opposing trait, the ability to sit and read and write happily. Hence, most salespeople, and sales managers, hate paperwork and reading; they are impatient and wiggly action people. ➤

Judge all your resume inclusions by your goal, so first you must have a goal.

Inclusion of any material should hereafter always be weighed against your goal for relevancy. If you want to be a train engineer, writing about your sales experience is ridiculous! Highlight your strengths and play down or omit your weaknesses. If you have a specific job or company in mind, you should know everything you can gather about your goal position before you write the resume. ➤

Gather facts by using this form.

One always searches out the facts before beginning any new project. Start by gathering the information on the following information sheet.

Resume and References Information Sheet

1. Your name, address and telephone number(s): (Use both home and business numbers!)

2. The name or title of the job you want (For example, computer programmer, civil engineer, sales representative. Perhaps there are several jobs you'd consider performing.)

3. Education (Include relevant seminars, special workshops, military training. Did you work your way through school?)

4. Honors/Activities (society memberships, awards, scholarships)

5. Hobbies (especially if they have to do with job) and community involvement

6. Special machines or equipment you operate (especially computers and software)

7. Job history (Work backwards giving the last job first.) Your job title, company name and location, dates (start/finish), description of duties, accomplishments. Continue as above until all jobs have been covered.

8. Qualifications you believe make you good for the job.

- Mechanical aptitude
- Quick to learn
- Work well under pressure
- Willingness to relocate and travel (very important)
- Responsible
- Prompt
- Good communicator
- Job experience

9. List of references

- Type these on a separate sheet that matches your resume.

- Include three to six people who know your work (past supervisors, co-workers, or customers for instance). They should be articulate people who could sell you should they be called. In other words, you select people for references who think you walk on water and will say so if they are called by a prospective employer!

- References are never given until asked for by a prospective employer. You don't want your reference people bothered otherwise.

- Ask your references for permission to include their names and tell them about your background. Most of us presume, incorrectly, that people know exactly what we do. ➤

Follow these step-by-step aids as you begin to write your resume.

Since being available is an obvious necessity, make sure your name (with certifications such as CPA, MD, CFP behind it), address, and the telephone numbers where you are most easily found are at the top of your resume. (I have seen resumes without names, addresses, or telephone numbers—but with explanations for wearing a toupee and not passing the bar exam). If you are difficult to reach, put an answering machine on your phone along with an answering tape that is well done and serious. This is not the time for clowns and impersonators to greet your callers! ➤

Use resume headings and goals that highlight your skills and serve you best.

There is no such thing as a general resume. Make sure your goal or job title is typed at the top so the reader quickly knows what you want. Goals can be broad, generic, or very specific. Remember that resumes are skimmed and that flowery, long-winded objectives so favored by academics are usually passed over quickly by the results-oriented decision maker. ➤

Check to be sure all vital information is easy to see.

I'm not alone in having read complete resumes without being able to tell what the people did that made a difference or what the job was they wanted. Look at these *real* resume headings (with names and numbers changed) of clients who found jobs.

Resume Heading Examples

1

Resume of JOHN R. ROGERS	7040 Holly Tree #321
	Anytown, USA 00000
Goal: Director of Program Operations	
and/or General Manager—Radio	214/555-5500

2

JOYCE M. HARRIS	13999 Montfort #254
	Anytown, USA 00000
SALES REPRESENTATIVE	214/555-3545

3

214/555-8966 (message)		6998 Delaplane
214/555-7599	JAMES SOUTH GERRICK	Anytown, USA 00000
	Goal: Technical Sales/Management Trainee	

JEANNINE ALLEN DOE, C.P.A.   214/555-3333
1111 Forest Drive #223, Anytown, USA 00000

214/555-7682 (H)   Rt. 3, Box 4494
214/555-2300 (W)   STEVEN B. HARRISON   Anytown, USA 00000
MANAGER OF PEOPLE AND PROPERTY

JOHN MAXWELL BARKSDALE   4947 Fallon Springs Dr.
                              Suite 2002, Anytown, USA 00000
      experience in   214/555-1100

SALES PROMOTIONAL & OPERATIONS MANAGEMENT
Market Analysis, Training, Investor Liaison

MARY LOUISE SMITH
3327 Dogwood Trail, Dallas, Texas 75221   214/334-4700

an experienced PROGRAMMING DIRECTOR
- ■ Researcher of Current Trends
- ■ Speaker and Fund Raiser
- ■ Creative Designer and Planner
- ■ Organizational Coordinator
- ■ Media and Public Relations Liaison
- ■ Manager and Trainer of Personnel

Weigh whether education or experience is stronger.

And the stronger of the two becomes the first category after the resume heading. Included under this heading are any relevant seminars or career development. (This keeps your resume uncluttered by avoiding too many headings.) ➤

Try this format if your degree is irrelevant.

Remember that over a third of us work in areas outside of our degree specialty. Handle that degree in biology when you are seeking sales work by omitting your major.

EDUCATION
B.S., MISSISSIPPI STATE UNIVERSITY, December 1983

➤

See if this works if your
degree was earned long ago.

If it has been a long time since you earned your degree, simply omit the graduation date.

Remember, your resume is an advertisement, not an affadavit!

Use your degree as a sales point if it is relevant.

(Two year degree with expanded coursework)

EDUCATION

A.A.S., Electronics, December 1983

SAN JOSE COLLEGE, San Antonio, Texas

Relevant coursework

- Systems Design
- Engineering Drawing
- Integrated Circuits
- Microprocessors
- Communications Equipment
- Computers
- Electronic Drafting
- Semiconductors
- Alternating Current
- Industrial Equipment
- Computer Graphics

TOOK ONE 21-HOUR SEMESTER WHILE MAINTAINING 3.0 GPA
DEAN'S LIST

➤

Try this approach if you have some college, but no four-year degree.

EDUCATION
UNIVERSITY OF NEBRASKA, Lincoln, and
UNIVERSITY OF MONTANA, Missoula
1980–84

---

or

Associate in Arts & Science, 1982, BUSINESS ADMINISTRATION
PINE VALLEY COLLEGE, Dallas, Texas

Support a position where
credentials matter with this
kind of styling.

(Two degrees and career development)

EDUCATION and PROFESSIONAL DEVELOPMENT

M.A., Psychology/Criminology, HOPKINS UNIVERSITY, Ames, IN, 1971
Currently working toward Ph.D., Psychology

B.S., Music Therapy/Psychology, UNIVERSITY OF TEXAS, Austin, 1964
Registered Music Therapist

Career Development/Professional Associations

- Motivation
- Self Defense
- Budgeting
- Body Language
- Managing Combative Clients

- Group, Individual, Family, & Therapy
- Care of Schizophrenia, Manic/Depression (Bi-Polar), Sociopathy

CHAIRPERSON, 12 years, National Clinical Training Division, National Association of Crime Fighters. Planned & directed national conferences.

➤

Play up your seminars and other career training you received while you were employed if you are a high school graduate only.

EDUCATION

Professional Development:

1986—Empowering Leadership
1985—Supervising Subordinates, Phases 1,2,3,4
1984—Managing Human Performance
1982—Financial Communications
1981—Communications Workshop

Graduate, Highland Park High School, Texas, 1980

Outline campus leadership roles in addition to education if you are an entry-level new college graduate.

Education

B.S. Cum Laude, Home Economics, May 1986

ARIZONA STATE UNIVERSITY, Tempe

Emphasis: Textiles and Clothing in Business Major GPA 3.3

LEADERSHIP ACTIVITIES/MEMBERSHIPS
- Co-Chair, Arizona State Homecoming Parade, fall 1983
- Treasurer, social sorority, spring 1982
- Member, Arizona Home Economics Association, fall 1984-1985

➤

Use this heading when you are a person with many years of diversified experience.

Your first section could be one that quickly outlines your qualifications in bullet form.

MARY LOUISE SMITH   214/555-2222 (work)
1111 Happywood Dr., Dallas, Texas 75222   214/555-1111 (home)

an experienced PROGRAMMING DIRECTOR

- Researcher of Current Trends
- Speaker and Fund Raiser
- Creative Designer and Planner
- Organizational Coordinator
- Media and Public Relations Liaison
- Manager and Trainer of Personnel

➤

Try an approach like this if you are a management executive.

STRENGTHS

EXPERIENCED in financial analysis, sales/marketing, purchasing and inventory control. Logical planner.

INTERPERSONAL SKILLS Optimistic. Act with integrity.

PROFIT-MINDED Articulate, convincing negotiator.

➤

Select a starting format like this if you are a complicated board chair or executive-level job seeker.

VALUE TO YOUR ORGANIZATION

HISTORY OF GENERATING BUSINESS for both public
and private firms, on Wall Street, throughout U.S., Canada,
Middle East

SENSITIVE TO ORGANIZATIONAL PROBLEMS AND
PEOPLE. Pragmatic understanding of business affairs.

➤

Try a qualifications summary if you are executive level.

PROFESSIONAL QUALIFICATIONS

OVER 14 YEARS P & L RESPONSIBILITY. Experience in developing and implementing overall business plans, market analysis, order and production forecasting, manpower and training needs, facilities and equipment, operating capital requirements.

BUILD TEAMWORK AND LOYALTY. Respect talent and professionalism. Persuasive. Unquestioned integrity.

BROAD CONTACTS. Extensively traveled. 12–14 weeks annually to Taiwan, Hong Kong, Japan, Europe.

➤

Scan this example if you are a

computer engineer.

VALUE TO YOUR ORGANIZATION

12 YEARS EXPERIENCE in design and implementation of processing systems. Inquiring mind with strong interests in symbolic programming, artificial intelligence.

COMMUNICATOR with background in training others.

SINGLE, WILLING TO RELOCATE and travel.

➤

Be aware of the four things decision makers most often seek in a candidate.

They are: experience, communication and interpersonal skills, the formal education needed for the job, and the flexibility to relocate. ➤

Center the section names on the page.

(Remember, we're going to place the important things on the left.) Don't underline those titles because we're going to save bolding and underlining for things that are important about you in order to draw the reader's eye to what needs to be seen quickly. ➤

Write a succinct job
description.

All facts should have bullets before them, and should begin with hard verbs that denote action. The job description is written in outline form, so you don't need to write complete sentences. Find ways to make this description of your job duties easily understood.

Write a job description for each of your jobs as you continue backwards through your work history, remembering to highlight those duties most supportive or illustrative of your goal. To understand how this might be done, you can quickly glance at some of the resume examples at the end of this chapter. Keep in mind that a resume is a quickly scanned advertisement, not an English theme. ➤

Group early positions if necessary.

Toward the end of your Career History or Experience section, you may decide to title several earlier but relevant jobs simply as Early Employment. List those jobs quickly to simply justify time or support your experience. Don't go back too many years, however, and leave this section off completely if it's irrelevant. ➤

Learn to write hooks.

Under each job description write as a hook the accomplishment that you are proudest of having done during that job period. Real hooks used on my clients' resumes include: "Recovered over $2,000 in accounts receivable monthly because of communication ability—1985," or "Persuasive—collected 20 overdue accounts company planned to write off." Or "Stayed on top of trends—business increased 40%, 1986." ➤

New Way #116

Think about using quotes from

evaluations as hooks.

Often past supervisors have said things about you that you could not say for yourself. What about this real review quote: "Your professionalism combined with your ability to recruit excellent people gave life to a program that never saw much success."

Construction people might simply list their specific projects as hooks. Financial managers can list all the areas of finance and accounting that they oversee. ➤

New Way #117

Always be positive.

Write about what you did, not what you did not do. Should personal information be relevant (though it seldom is), *divorced* becomes *single*.

(By the way, personal information such as height, weight, and age is relevant only if you are an actor, flight attendant, or in some other profession where appearance is part of your sell.) ➤

Do not include salary history
or why you left a previous job.

This is an inviolable rule. Highlighting details in these areas can *only* screen you out, and can *never* screen you in. ➤

Think of placing job titles on the left side of the page if you've had several jobs.

Then add hooks on the right to pull the eye to real, memorable accomplishments.

PROFESSIONAL EXPERIENCE

INTAKE WORKER/CASE MANAGER, Anytown (USA) Regional Mental Health & Mental Rehabilitation, 1984-Present
- Participated in group & family therapy
- Saw clients; updated current cases
- Made presentations at weekly staff meeting

Case manager for mentally ill adults, working closely with state hospital to set up community help for discharges

CHILD CARE WORKER, YMCA Juvenile Justice Dept., Anytown, 1981-84
(Clients referred through Probation Department, agencies, families)
- Made home visits; charted regularly weekly contracts with youth about personal, home, and school life
- Learned workings of Anytown legal system

Provided daily intake, assessment, scheduling and activity direction of youth ages 6-16

INTERN, Family Outreach of Anytown, 1980
- Home visits and telephone counseling
- Arranged for services, clothing, food

Child abuse prevention case management

Select a format like this if

you have had many positions

with one company.

EXPERIENCE

BLACKSTONE DEPARTMENT STORES, Anytown, USA, 1979-86

Served in the following departments:

INVENTORY CONTROL, 1983-86
- Provided sales support for 16 stores
- Contacted salespeople regarding stock problems, customers about nondelivery of merchandise

ACCOUNTS PAYABLE, 1983
- Corrected and approved invoices and receiver printouts for incoming merchandise prior to payment
- Liaison with buyers and vendors

CASH OFFICE CUSTOMER SERVICE, 1981-83
- Reconciled cash sales audits; solved merchandise, account and credit problems
- Cashiered charge accounts and checks
- Worked closely with security

MERCHANDISE/WAREHOUSE CREDIT SERVICE, 1979-80
- Handled authorization, new accounts, collections, and returned checks by telephone
- Walk-in customer service

INITIATED TALLY SYSTEM to track customer calls

COMPUTER EXPERIENCE:
- Took down system for all stores nightly and ran programs
- Entered and corrected ticket sales for all stores daily
- Checked all inventories
- Generated all reports

70% CUSTOMER SERVICE for largest retail cash office in southwest U.S.

WON AWARD—OPENED 1000 CHARGE ACCOUNTS IN 15
MONTHS—most in company history

AUTHORED CREDIT TRAINING MANUAL detailing methods for settle-
ment of large ticket charge account problems

➤

Try this if you have had too

many jobs.

Sometimes you can group them to make that fact less obvious.

CAREER HISTORY

MECHANICAL SYSTEM DEVELOPMENT, SALES & INSTALLATION,
1982-Present
- ■ DENMANN FARMS, INC., Dallas, Iowa, 1984-1986
  Oversaw all facets of project, including payroll and
  supervision of 24-person crew
- ■ THOMAS W. JEROME FACILITIES, Ives, Ohio, 1982-84
  Developed 2,000-head hog feeding system using
  economical whey
  Managed construction & start-up of unique $2,100,000
  computerized feeding system

OVERSEAS SALES/PROMOTION, 1972-82
- ■ BREEDER CATTLE COMPANY, Columbus, Iowa, 1980-82
  Located buyers, coordinated shipping, arranged letters of
  credit for 1800 breeding stock
- ■ JEROME HYBRID SEED CO., Ives, Ohio, 1972-80
  Developed markets in Latin America
  Set up dealer organization

➤

Do this if you are turning over into a new field, have had too many jobs, or find yourself weak for any reason.

Sometimes listing hooks close to that strong left side of the page draws the reader's eye away from the fact that your jobs haven't been as relevant as you would like.

COMBAT COMMUNICATIONS, Minneapolis, Cleveland, and Chicago, 1975-present

Value to Your Organization:

ENJOY GIVING SALES FORCE RESULTS... **HELPING PEOPLE** "She is quick ... an outstanding job ... coordinated move ... without problems." Evaluation, 1988

LISTENER ABLE TO CALM IRATE CUSTOMERS & ".. able to maintain her focus on the job at hand ..." Evaluation, 1989

STAFF SUPERVISOR-SALES CLERICAL SUPPORT, 1983-date

SUPERVISE, interview, develop, motivate, review, delegate, and schedule staff of 6-11 at 2 sites

PROVIDE LIAISON BETWEEN SALES MANAGER AND SUPPORT STAFF to coordinate clerical needs, such as bid and proposal preparation

DEAL WITH OUTSIDE VENDORS

COORDINATE LOCAL TRAINING; establish skills levels and improvement plans
 • Set up recognition program for clerical staff
 • Coordinated training of 150 marketing personnel

OVERSEE ADMINISTRATIVE FUNCTIONS, such as employee benefits, EEO/AAP plans, safety and health plans, time reporting, payroll, transfers, union matters

SOLVE PROBLEMS. "This employee set up a system utilizing each rental car which saved $15,000 in one year."

➤

**Realize that the more you know
about the person and company
where your resume will be seen,
the better your resume will be.**

It's called "qualifying" in sales: finding and filling needs. And
this is sales, remember. You are the product. ➤

Know the best methods for

leaving your resume.

The best resume is the one left behind after you have talked with someone informally, perhaps at a social gathering. Then you can call on that person again to leave the resume and familiarize him or her with your business background.

The second-best resume is the one somebody else carries in for you (with a little sales pitch, hopefully; they can say things you could never say for yourself).

Third best is the resume you take with you to the interviewer so that you and the resume arrive together; that's the one the decision maker reads at the time you also are present to make an impression.

Fourth best is the one you mail with a cover letter after you have spoken with the decision maker on the telephone and have been told to send it. Even then, you should do everything possible to deliver the resume in person. Say, "I'm going to be on your side of town late tomorrow. I'll drop it by and say hello if you are in." If the resume must be mailed because the prospective employer is located outside of your area, then send it in a different way—by special mail service or to someone inside you've gotten to know on the telephone (who can then hand carry it to the decision maker).

The next to worst way to employ a resume is to use it to answer an advertisement or to send it to a head hunter or personnel agency.

The worst use of a resume is to mail it out cold to some sort of list. ➤

Read this real story of how to get directly to a decision maker.

Sue was working for a nonprofit organization and oversaw work in seven large counties. Even so, as often happens in nonprofit positions, she worked more for love than for money. Sue called one day from a nearby town and told me she'd heard of a job in a nearby city for an agency that paid double her present salary. Could I see her and help update her resume quickly?

Late in the day Sue arrived, and I insisted that she call the agency about their opening. (Always call—almost every time you'll gain valuable information.) After calling she returned to my office and told me that "the snippy little girl who answered the phone" told her that the director was accepting nothing but resumes with cover letters, and he already had seventy! Sue was downcast. What could we do?

We finished updating her resume and wrote a quick cover letter (in order to make everyone feel comfy). Then I instructed her, since it was already late in the day, to go to their offices, wait in the hall until five o'clock or until the snippy little girl left, and walk in. Since this was a start-up situation, I reasoned that it would be likely that the decision maker would be alone. He was. This gave Sue time to be personally identified by the decision maker and to become memorable as a real person—something the seventy other applicants who had sent in could not do. She got the job. ➤

Know what to do if you are referred to Personnel by a decision maker.

But, you ask, what if the prospective employer sends me to the Personnel Department (or to Human Resources) to be interviewed?

My answer is for you to understand that you have been sent "from above;" just that simple fact will help you stand out from the crowd. The Personnel interviewer *knows* you are supposed to be interviewed. Responsibility for the hiring is shared with the decision maker, which takes a little of the fear for making a mistake off Personnel if you don't fit the decision maker's original job description or recipe. ➤

Don't expect prospective employers to favor you with a reply after you've mailed a resume or been interviewed.

That's just unrealistic behavior today for several reasons. First, just placing an advertisement now can result in dozens, sometimes hundreds of resumes and cover letters. That's one of the reasons that answering ads is so unproductive. Second, most companies simply no longer keep enough staff to reply to all inquiries. Third, like it or not, in a world that is terrifically competitive and results oriented, manners and ethics frequently take a back seat to expediency. ➤

University: LAUREN J. APPLELET   Permanent:
1212 Tillis #222   P.O. Box 7011
Austin, TX 78700   Carrollton, TX 75000
                   B.B.A, ACCOUNTING, December 1990
512/222-2222   214/222-2222

Education

**While working to earn
60-70% of college
education, maintained:**

UNIVERSITY OF TEXAS, at Austin
21 hours Accounting
HONORS/ACTIVITIES:

* **3.37 Overall GPA**
* **3.66 Accounting
  GPA**
* **4.0 Richland GPA**

* Dean's Honor Roll, 1985-86
* Member, University Accounting Association
* Intramural Softball
* Student Representative, United Action for the Elderly, 1986-87

CPA, November, 1990

* President's Honor Roll, Richland College, 1984-85
* Graduated in top 10%, Richardson High School

Skills:

* **10-key**
* **IBM PC**

Work To Defray College Expenses

**Through these jobs
learned:**

JORRY DESIGNS, Austin, 1985-present
(Wholesale jewelry kiosk shows in mall)

**Dependability; rarely
absent**

* Recruit and train up to 23 employees
* Aid in production; set up shows
* Inventory control, bookkeeping, reporting

**Accuracy under time
pressures**

BLUE TEXAS STAR CAFE, Austin, 1985
(20 hours weekly)

**To work with team or
independently**

* Trusted to balance register, prepare daily cash sheet, vendor payouts

**Initiative; to see what
needs to be done**

NEIMAN-MARCUS, Dallas, 1984-85
(20 hours weekly) Sales/Inventory

**To respond quickly
and analytically**

DAVID D. DAVID, Attorney, Dallas, 1984
(full time, summer) Receptionist and Assistant in setting up new real estate law office

**Flexibility; willing to
travel**

LORD & TAYLOR, Dallas, 1982-84, summer
1986 Sales/Inventory (full & part time)

References on request

GLENDA T. GEORGIA 214/222-2222 (O)
222 Federal #22, Dallas, TX 22222 214/322-2222 (H)

Goal: SOFTWARE TRAINING and/or MARKETING SUPPORT
Willing to relocate and travel

Career History
COMPUTERS UNLIMITED, Dallas, TX, 1983-present

MARKETING REPRESENTATIVE, Aug. 1986-date
- Sell microcomputers (IBM, Compaq, Apple) and related peripherals and software, principally to small businesses
- Target markets; demonstrate, prepare and present proposals; manage accounts

Cited by supervisor for positive attitude, quickness, leadership ... energetic "team player"

MARKETING SUPPORT REPRESENTATIVE, 1984-86
- Provided technical sales assistance and software demonstrations to marketing representatives and prospective customers
- Trained clients in software package use (Lotus, MultiMate, Symphony, dBase, DOS, WordStar, DataEase, and Framework II)
- Served as liaison between sales force and vendor representatives, including IBM, Microsoft, Ashton-Tate, Compaq and Apple
- Software/hardware problem solver between customers and service technicians

Long-term assignments include teaching Lotus and MultiMate classes while providing on-going support at Rothchild Medical Center, Dallas

Enjoy helping people, maintaining excellent customer service

MARKETING ASSISTANT, 1983-84
- Oversaw all product invoicing on POS system, running daily inventory and sales reports
- Provided information to customers and prospects; developed customer mailing list

Assisted in creating and managing store database

Education
B.S., 1981, UNIVERSITY OF MONTANA, Missoula
Journalism/Spanish Dean's List

Career Development: Compaq Product Training, Apple Dealer Training, Ashton-Tate, MultiMate, dBase, Lotus 1-2-3, Businessland Sales Training

References on request

MARION M. JONES, B.S., R.R.T.   214/555-5555
2244 Smith Drive, Keller, Texas 75000

RESPIRATORY THERAPIST Experience
- Mechanical ventilation
- Emergency life support
- IPPB, CPT, EKGs, tracheal aspiration
- Aerosol and ultrasonic nebulizer treatments
- Arterial puncture and blood gas analysis
- Instruction

Ultimate Goal: Management and Teaching

Career History

FULL-TIME EXPERIENCE
Carrolltown Medical Center
Cardiopulmonary Services
401 W. Campbell Rd., Carrolltown, TX 75080
214/222-2222. June 1986-present

Adult intensive care and general therapy in 250-bed broad spectrum facility.

Rothchild Medical Center
Pulmonary Medicine Department
1935 Amelia St., Keller, TX 75235
214/220-2222. Nov. 1984-June 1986 (Current part time)

Emergency care of children. Instructed parents, patients, and staff in CPR, home therapy equipment, and medications.

INTERIM AND COLLEGE EMPLOYMENT
Southern Memorial Hospital
Cardiopulmonary Department
2200 W. Illinois, South, TX 79701
915/111-1111

Broad spectrum work in general hospital (during family illness).

Ohio State University
School of Allied Medical Professions
Respiratory Therapy Division
1588 Perry St., Columbus, OH 43210
614/433-3333. May 1983-May 1984

Extensive experience in the medical, surgical, burn, and neurosurgical intensive care units of 1000-bed, tertiary care facility.

Education
B.S., Allied Health Professions, OHIO STATE UNIVERSITY, 1984
Respiratory Therapy major Summa Award recipient
Department Management/Critical Care specialization

Texas License, NBRC-Registered Respiratory Therapist
AHA-CPR Instructor, AARC and TSRC member

References on request

Resume of **GEORGIA A. (G. A.) TOLBERT**

Goal: Administrative or Sales Support

200 Springcrest Dr.
Groves, TX 22222
214/222-2222

Career History

ADMINISTRATIVE
A.B.C. Temporaries, Inc., Dallas, 6/85-Present (Full time)
- WORD PROCESSING/typing (75-85 wpm)
- ACCOUNTING/bookkeeping (10-key by touch)
- DATA ENTRY (IBM-PC/Lotus 1-2-3 & WordStar)

Office operations work during college.

Directed credit and contract approvals. Organized office to be able to wrap up after-sales paperwork in 1 week instead of 3 to 4 in the past.

Family business (name on request), Irving, TX 1983-85
Involved in all administrative operations aspects of 18,000 sq. ft. retail furniture showroom
- INVENTORY CONTROL and purchasing
- SALES PROMOTIONS, floor sales, advertising liaison
- COLLECTIONS, A/R, A/P, bookkeeping

Managed 3 clerks as A/R, A/P Supervisor.

Tors Reinsurance Company Dallas, 1978-79
- ORGANIZED to save money by meeting discount deadlines, pay executive expenses within 24 hours

Handled details of sale/purchase of stocks and bonds for 7 offices in 3 states.

Jones, Able, and Burnett, Stockbrokers, Dallas 1975-78
Accounts Payable/Receivable Clerk, Acting Supervisor overseeing General Ledger

Employers' quotes:
"in top 10% of 68 ... intense preparation ... combination of brains and hard work. Grown up in business ... started selling at 12. Distinct executive potential."

SALES
Jones & Does, Inc., Dallas, 1981-83
Office systems Dallas/DFW Area Sales Representative (mailing systems, inserters, collators, etc.)
- SALES AND PRODUCT USAGE TRAINER in several positions

Education

Work toward **ACCOUNTING DEGREE** (90 hours—12/87), U.T. at Dallas
Career Development: Texas Real Estate Sales License, Selling Skills, Fitney Dowes, Zig Zigler & Tom Hopkins

References on request

WILLIAM H. ROSEN

2222 North 79th West, Washington, DC 22222   222/222-2222

TECHNICAL SALES and SERVICE MANAGER
- OVER 14 YEARS EXPERIENCE
- TEAM LEADER who has hired and/or supervised up to 19 personnel
- TRAINER of 250+ personnel; persuasive communicator
- BUDGET, forecasting, and project implementation background
- FLEXIBLE DELEGATOR who inspires loyalty and job performance
- PROFITABILITY ORIENTED; good under deadline pressures

Career, Educational, and Personal Data

U.S. SERVICE MANAGER AND SALES ENGINEER, DYNAMIC

Opened new worldwide markets, assessed customer needs, adapted machinery and trained staff; coordinated efforts through local offices.

INDUSTRIES INTERNATIONAL, Vienna, Austria (1981-84) and Washington (1978-81 and 1984-87)

- Represented Dynamo products
- Conducted training for Eimco personnel and mine site crews
- Supervised tests at mine sites to improve equipment productivity and adapt machinery to special applications

Sold over $20M in new equipment, generating thousands more in spare parts and consumables.

- Planned and developed repair shop for hydraulic equipment
- Coordinated spare part reconditioning and automatic parts reordering system, as well as consumable manufacture
- Improved inventory costs (use computer)

"Gregarious personality ... well like by ... customers and his fellow workers." 1984

- Commendation quote: "few truly outstanding contributors . . . your willingness to go the extra distance and achieve results well beyond normal expectations." 1985

RESEARCH AND DEVELOPMENT/SERVICE REPRESENTATIVE,

DYNAMO, Vienna, Austria 1974-78

Introduced over 60 pieces of equipment, modifying to meet client needs.

- Field tested and improved hydraulic percussive hammer, anti- jamming device, and automated resin injection roof bolting turret

Increased spare parts sales 20%.

- Developed training programs for operators and maintenance crews

B.S., CHEMISTRY/PHYSICS, 1968, VIENNA JESUIT, Austria; biology minor

Seminars include "Communication Under Stress" & "Hydraulics."

- Military: extensive training in cooling systems and hydraulics. Supervised six.
- Speak fluent German, English, Spanish.

References on request

LUKE AVON LUCKEY, C.P.A.

2222 Central Expressway, Avon, Ohio 22222   222/222-2222

FINANCIAL MANAGEMENT EXECUTIVE

Career History

VICE PRESIDENT/FINANCE, (company name on request), Avon, Ohio, 1976-present ($45M annual sales distributor of consumer appliances; real estate)

HEAD ALL FINANCIAL OPERATIONS—Plan internal controls to provide asset safety, prompt collections, increased inventory turnover, cost reductions, product line profitability, audit programs, and analysis of growth or divestment depending on changing profit margin or market.
* Reduced delinquency rate 30-40%; strengthened credit procedures.

MANAGE PERSONNEL—Direct Controller, 15 accounting personnel
* Team leader who gains loyalty quickly, juggles projects and deadlines.

IMPLEMENT CASH MANAGEMENT PROGRAMS—Reduce interest cost and improve cash forecasting.
* Negotiate with banks for term financing; long-term credit lines with savings and loans and asset-based lenders.

DEVELOP ON-LINE DATA PROCESSING SYSTEM—Honeywell mainframe; personally use PC/Lotus 1-2-3 for financial and cash planning, budgeting, and measuring investment return.

OVERSEE RISK MANAGEMENT/PENSION FUND
* Decreased cost of life and casualty insurance 30%. Reviewed and combined policies for greater coverage at lower cost.
* Evaluate and compare pension fund bank and investment performance.

PLAN INVESTMENT STRATEGIES
* Serve on estate and corporate planning team. Review and recommend changes to portfolio, evaluating investments for fifteen family trusts.

DEVELOP CORPORATE REORGANIZATION
* Avoid corporate tax consequences by eliminating personal holding company, forming partnership and Sub S.

Early employment includes financial Vice President for two insurance companies, and computer software firm. Began with Big 8 accounting firm.

EDUCATION

B.B.A., Accounting/Management Analysis, Southern Methodist University
C.P.A., 1978—AICPA, State and Dallas

References on request

JOSE SILVA-RODRIQUEZ   222/222-2222
                    2222 Ferndale Drive, Houston, TX 22222

Goal: OPERATIONS OR FINANCIAL MANAGER/ANALYST

Education
B.B.A. FINANCE, Cum Laude, UNIVERSITY OF TEXAS at Austin
Dean's List every semester. Maintained 3.5 GPA while finishing coursework in
three years and working full time each summer. Active in business and honor
societies.

Career History

FINANCIAL/LEGAL/OPERATIONS ANALYST, Houston Industries, Inc., TX
1988-present (Largest independent steel fabricator and
processor in U.S.—$110M in annual revenue)

Working independently and interfacing with corporate
executive management:
- In-depth analysis and forecasting of steel pur-
  chases and utility usage systemwide
- Track systemwide sales
- Supported purchasing services for glass and
  long-distance voice carriers for all plants
- Summarized all insurance provisions of contracts

**Developed computerized
steel tracking system to
centralize purchasing for
15 plants. Use IBM-AT
(Novell Network)—Excel,
Quattro, Lotus, Javelin,
WordPerfect.**

**Create financial models
for executive
management.**

**Summarized all financing
documents to verify
covenant requirements.**

DIRECTOR OF FINANCE AND ACCOUNTING, Everett Electronics, Inc.,
Houston, TX, 1985-1988 (mfg. of security metal detectors)

- Hired/fired/trained/disciplined/reviewed   and
  scheduled A/R, A/P, payroll and order-entry employees
- Administered/invested profit sharing plan; managed cash
- Analyzed sales trends, product costs, wages and
  salaries, shipping and order tracking
- Represented department at weekly staff meetings
- Negotiated freight, traffic, customs

**Responsible for all
financial management:
* Analysis
* Reporting
* Budgeting
* Personnel
* Risk Management
* Letters Of Credit
* Banking
* Month-end Closing
* Collections
* Liaison With CPA,
Attorneys, Bankers**

Career history continued, page 2

Career history continued

HOUSTON OPERATIONS COORDINATOR/FINANCIAL ANALYST,
Iceland Distributors, 1983-85 (Import/Export)

- Developed financial accounting systems using IBM-PC
- Managed office
- Coordinated international transfers of funds and merchandise
- Traveled overseas
- Prepared bank loan presentations

Developed corporate budget, cash flow models, sales projections.

Introduced new product to Texas markets, beginning with Neiman-Marcus's English Festival.

Employment during schooling:

ASSISTANT FINANCIAL ANALYST
Toy Petroleum, Houston, Summers 1981-82. Supervised one.

- Assisted on capital budget
- Began as Accounting Assistant

Helped coordinate limited partnership "roll-up" for sale of units on American Stock Exchange.

SALES, Neiman-Marcus/Houston, Menswear, 1979-81

Often in top 10 (of 70) in sales even during school year.

Career Development and Community Affiliations

Europe 1992, American Bar Association, 1989 (Open discussion with top officials of the European community)
Expertise with Letters of Credit, U.S. Department of Commerce, 1988
How to Bid to Governments, (2 days), Austin, 1988
Import/Export Financing, International Chamber Committee, 1987
Doing Business in a Global Economy, Dallas Chamber of Commerce, 1987
Time Management, Steve Klein, Dallas Chamber of Commerce, 1986

Guest Speaker/Committee Member, International Committee on Small Business, Dallas Chamber of Commerce, 1987-88

The 500 Inc., Houston Services for Visually Impaired Children

References on request

MARIA LONGWORTH SMITH   222/222-2222
2222 Washington, Chicago, IL 22222

Goal: Recruiter/Coordinator

Value To Your Organization

EXPERIENCE WITH TEXAS MARKET CENTER aiding in designing, developing, promoting, and implementing entertainment, special events, and educational seminars to generate market attendance.

COMMUNICATOR AND LIAISON. Can interview, research, write and speak publicly. Speak and write Spanish. Accustomed to making travel arrangements. Attractive professional appearance.

WORK AS PART OF TEAM OR WITH MINIMAL SUPERVISION; problem solver who prioritizes quickly.

HANDLE TASK DETAILS such as preparing brochures, schedules, and mailings; planning food, entertainment, speakers, and decorations; assisting in $500K budget forecasting and tracking; monitoring supplies and inventory.

Career History

Licensing Assistant/Agent Liaison, A & B MARKETING GROUP, Reno, NV Jan. 1989-present (markets life and health insurance)
Public Relations/Special Events Assistant, TEXAS MARKET CENTER COMPANY, Austin, TX, June to October 1988
Office Associate, TWICE DISTRIBUTING COMPANY, Reno, NV, Nov. 1987-June 1988
Assistant Manager/Salesperson, HOPEWELL & YOUNG, Reno, NV, January to November 1987 (retail apparel store)

Education and Affiliations

B.S., THE UNIVERSITY OF NEVADA, December 1986
Speech/Organizational Communication major
Worked to defray complete college expenses

Additional Courses: Radio/Television/Film (18 hours)
Career Development: IBM-PC, DOS, and word processing, Computerland (Type 60-70 wpm)
Local Affiliations: Nevada Alumni, Reno Young Republicans, March of Dimes (Gourmet Gala)
Personal Data: Willing to travel. Enjoy outdoor sports.

References on request

FLORENCE SMITH BLACKWOOD

222/111-1111 (H)   2222 East Western Hwy. #2222   222/222-2222 (O)
Dallas, Texas 22222

PROFESSIONAL HISTORY

Sales, Marketing, and Administrative Experience

Ace Business Travel And Ace World Business Incentives, Dallas, 1987-88

Brought in accounts with annual volume from $100k to $25m, proving money can be made in Texas bust Following dissolution of Dallas division of Sun and Crabstreet, joined ABT to handle top accounts. Negotiated with airlines, hotels, car rental agencies, cruise lines, and tour companies for cost effective planning for both agency and clients.

Sun & Crabstreet, McAppley Information Publishing sub., Irving, TX, 1985-86.

Advanced from #45 to top producer within six months, while directing entire support staff. Recruited to sell McAppley Directory, two other publications to top revenue accounts. Oversaw marketing, art, copy, and staff. "She is a very hard working, aggressive and most capable young lady." Quote from Assistant Vice President.

Marketing and Start-up Business Consulting Projects

ARRANGED DISPLAY PACKAGES for John Bonwit, famed artist, 1985-87

PLANNED PROMOTIONAL PACKAGES that placed Doggie Love, Inc., in famous retailers catalogs, on Johnny Carson Show, 1986

RAISED FUNDS and syndicated investment packages in land, oil, film, importing/exporting, Florence Smith, Inc., 1984

ARRANGED SPECIAL TRAVEL and entertainment events for top clientele, as Texas representative for Las Vegas hotel, 1983

DESIGNED COMPLETE FUR LINE. Bought furs and marketed in Canada, U.S., Mexico, Hong Kong, Alaska, Florence Smith Furs, 1983

FOUNDED/MANAGED PLACEMENT FIRM for models, entertainers, actors, and musicians, Florence Smith Talent, 1981-83

BOOKED U.S. TOURS, scheduled, negotiated for travel for entertainers, Concerts Now, 1978-80

PREPARED CORPORATE BACKGROUND RESEARCH as Licensed Private Investigator, Jeffries and Love Detective Agency, 1976-77

FREELANCE MODEL/Corporate Film Actress, 1962-81, Texas and overseas

Education and Personal Data

UNIVERSITY OF MIAMI, 1972-75. Social science/psychology graduate, 1971, INCARNATE WORD ACADEMY FOR GIRLS, Houston

References on request   Willing to travel

Know that writing a cover letter and mailing a resume is a last resort.

You should first have tried to talk with the decision maker on the telephone and hand deliver the resume. You should also have built rapport with someone inside the company (the prospective employer's secretary, the investor relations representative, or a social acquaintance) to whom you can take or mail your resume, so they can hand deliver it for you. ➤

Understand when you must write

a cover letter.

Consider mailing only when you have been unable to stop by to hand deliver the resume, could find no friend of the decision maker to take it in for you, or the company office is too far away to make any of the above practical. Here are some helpful guidelines.

In the very first paragraph, use a recognizable name as a hook to the reader's attention, if at all possible. This is a way of making the benefactor/networking system work for you. "As you may recall from our telephone conversation last Tuesday, Mary Ann Jones told me to call you," or, "John Brown recommended that I talk with you about openings in computer sales." (This technique works equally well on the telephone.)

Use the title of the job or area you want at the beginning of your letter, also. "Re: Project Manager," or "A resume highlighting my construction management experience is enclosed."

Prepare the reader for the sell that is coming with a sentence (still part of the first paragraph) such as, "Please note on the enclosed resume the following assets I could bring to your organization." or "I know I could quickly become a productive member of your team because of the following . . ."

Then indent and highlight three or four bulletted items that seemed to grab him/her when you spoke on the phone.

Your closing paragraph could read: "Mr. Jones, I would appreciate a personal interview. I am visiting the Annapolis area July 15-23. I can be reached at the number below, or I will give you a call in a couple of weeks to work out a convenient time for us to meet." ➤

Grab the reader's eye quickly
with a cover letter.

The major criteria for a good cover letter is one that makes the reader's eye travel to what you want him/her to see by using indented bullets to support your goal. (If you want to be considered a fool, you'll include some flowery verbiage about how much you'd like to work for such a wonderful company. Remember, the reader is already inside the company and knows it's practically never wonderful in these days of mergers, takeovers, and downsizing.) ➤

Add a handwritten P.S.

Do this if you have something you really want the reader to notice. I guarantee you that the P.S. will be the very first thing the reader sees. You might save your best selling point to put in the P.S. ➤

Scan some of these cover letters to find ideas that fit your situation.

These cover letters have been slightly changed to protect the innocent, but are versions of real ones used successfully by my clients. ➤

John Henry Brown, C.P.A.
2222 Maple Leaf
Hico, Texas 22222
214/422-2222

February 17, 1991

Mr. Aston Martin
Martin Financial
22 E. Tower Avenue
Chicago, IL 60666

Re: Vice President
finance position

Dear Mr. Martin:

Presently employed as vice president/finance, I meet the qualifications you discussed with our mutual friend, Mable Able, down to the last detail. Please note on the enclosed resume:

OVERSEE ALL TREASURY AND CONTROLLERSHIP FUNCTIONS
- Financial statement preparation, accounting
- Management planning, analysis, and reporting
- Investments; short and long term, equities and fixed income
- Budgeting, control, auditing
- Banking; short-term credit, long-term and asset-based financing
- Information systems supervision
- Tax, audit, and risk management

EXPERIENCED IN CORPORATE RESTRUCTURING AND NEW VENTURES
- Acquisition/divestiture search, analysis, and assimilation

COMMUNICATOR, LEADER AND EXECUTIVE TEAM MEMBER
- Build corporate spirit and loyalty while managing complete CFO functions and organization
- Use computers for financial planning, cash flow, budgeting, analytical presentation, and interpretation
- Goal oriented. Organize people and tasks to set and reach objectives by developing business plans

Mr. Martin, I would appreciate time for an interview to discuss the expertise I could bring to your organization. I can be reached at the above number, or I will call you within the next week.

Sincerely,

John Henry Brown

For answering an advertisement—a *very long* (five percent) shot. Please don't spend much time doing these.

Matthew A. Bright, C.P.A.
2222 Harry Hines
Dallas, Texas 22222

214/222-2222 (H)
214/111-1111 (W)

January 28, 1990

Mr. W. C. Love—Accounting Division
STB Personnel Services
P.O. Box 22222
Houston, Texas 77222

Re: Financial Manager
position

Dear Mr. Love:

As you may recall from our telephone conversation last week, I fit ALL the qualifications indicated in your advertisement. At your request, my resume is enclosed. Please note that my experience includes:

Serve presently on acquisition negotiation team

C.P.A. with big 8 background—for over 5 years

Work with many corporate environments, including distribution through present position with 35-40 affiliated companies

Computer modeling and analysis experience

Work quickly but thoroughly to wrap-up and complete projects

Mr. Love, I am seeking a move to a Houston-area position. I would appreciate time for an interview to discuss my assets and background with you personally, and I can be reached at the above numbers. Should I fail to hear within a week, I'll contact you.

Sincerely,

Matthew A. Bright

(Letter when given a name by a benefactor)

JUNE APRIL SUMMERS
722 Winters Avenue
Faland, Ohio 22222

222/222-2222

August 18, 1988

Mr. Tom Spring, Regional Manager
X.Y.Z., Inc.
2222 Abrams
Heaven, PA 22222-2222

Dear Mr. Spring:

Ms. Diana Swoon, an X.Y.Z. General Manager in Austin, Texas, indicated that I should contact you directly to introduce myself and to present my qualifications. I believe my successful experiences as a Corporate Buyer, Merchandiser, and Product Developer could quickly make me an asset to your company.

Please note on the enclosed resume:

OVER 12 YEARS EXPERIENCE in buying, marketing, merchandising, sales, and management

RAPID PROGRESSION FROM DEPARTMENT STORE TO CORPORATE

HEAD MARKETING TEAM OF FOUR

WILLING TO RELOCATE AND TRAVEL

HOLD B.S., BUSINESS ADMINISTRATION

Armed with experience, loyalty, and the desire to be the best, I am more than capable of meeting the challenges of the future in hope of reaching my potential for significant professional achievement.

Mr. Spring, thank you for your consideration and confidentiality. I would appreciate the chance to discuss employment opportunities with you directly. I can be reached at the above address and number, or I will give you a call in a week or so.

Sincerely,

June A. Summers

(Another cover letter after generating a remote lead)

John Henry Morris
2222 E. Puppet Lane
New York, NY 22222

222/222-2222

June 17, 1990

Mr. Dick Shearer, Vice President of Marketing
Stromberg Furniture Designs
222 Fifth Avenue, Suite 222
Warren, Ohio 33333

Dear Mr. Shearer:

Warren Page, an old friend, asked me to mail my resume to you as a candidate for a position in sales with Stromberg Furniture Designs.

Please note these highlights:

FIFTEEN YEARS SUCCESSFUL SALES EXPERIENCE and exposure to the best while working at Neiman-Marcus

STRONG LONG-TERM INTEREST IN PERIOD FURNISHINGS sharpened by visits to Europe during Naval service

Mr. Shearer, I know I could bring an eagerness and enthusiasm to your organization that would be economically beneficial to both of us.

I will be visiting the Ohio area during the first week in September, and I would appreciate the opportunity for an interview. I can be reached at the above number, or I'll give you a call in a few days.

Sincerely yours,

John H. Morris

(Written as a follow-up after a telephone call)

Jennifer R. Fontenot
22 Scottsdale Circle
New Orleans, LA 23335

222/666-6666

March 13, 1990

Ms. Jane Doe, Marketing Manager
Ft. Worth City Hotels
2222 Main Street
Ft. Worth, TX 76666 Re: Marketing Coordinator
position

Dear Ms. Doe:

Thank you for the time you took from your busy day to talk with me yesterday, since I'm anxious to return to the hospitality industry.

As requested, my resume is enclosed. Please note these assets, with support quotes from supervisory and customer evaluations, that I could bring to your team.

Over five years hospitality industry experience. "Jennifer made sure the event worked smoothly and was handled professionally and courteously! When I think of her, I think of a top-notch hotel."

Quick and conscientious. "Flexible with changes and last- minute requests" (company name). "Extremely helpful" (company name). "Enthusiastic, positive . . . initiative and enthusiasm." "She followed through on everything she promised" (association name).

Strong interpersonal skills. "Jennifer, thanks for earning us another friend!" "Handled a multitude of tasks both courteously and efficiently." (company name).

Creative event designer. "Unforgettable events, due in large part to the expert planning and creative touches." "Arrangements entirely to our specifications with a minimum of activity on our part" (institution name).

Ms. Doe, could I talk with you again about the possibility of working with you at City Hotels? I can be reached at the above number, or I'll give you a call again in a few days.

Sincerely,

Jennifer Fontenot

(Contact from a head hunter)

John K. Brown
6666 Eveningside Avenue
Eramus, Pennsylvania 22222

222/222-2222

May 22, 1990

Ms. Jayne R. White
White and Associates
2222 Main Street
New York, NY 00000

Dear Ms. White:

I apologize for the delay in forwarding my confidential resume, but unfortunately I did not have a current resume prepared at the time of our conversation.

As we discussed on the phone, Jayne, I have a wide variety of sales and sales management experience with two large and respected firms. Besides this experience, I also have done extensive work as a sales trainer and market planner.

I intend to capitalize on that experience with a smaller and more aggressive young company.

In my current position, I represent my organization to large financial institutions on the East Coast. This involves working with the senior executives (CEO, CFO, Chairmen, and Directors) in the acquisition of long-term, multi-million dollar contracts for our services. These sales are long-term team efforts in which I play the role of a team captain who must manage his own internal company resources and employees, as well as those of the prospect. My quota for 1990 is $2 million, which I have already exceeded!

I hope that we have the opportunity to work together, Jayne. I look forward to again hearing from you.

Sincerely,

John K. Brown

(College student for summer job)

JOHN HENRY BROWNING

University:
2222 San Jacinto
Houston, TX 78777
512/777-7777

Permanent:
2222 Jocylyn Dr.
Dallas, TX 75222
214/222-2222

May 27, 1990

Ms. Jane Doe
Jones, Smith, and Doe
2222 Akard Street
Dallas, TX 752222

Dear Ms. Doe:

Thank you for speaking to me last Thursday about a clerk/messenger or other summer position with your firm. Please note these details on the enclosed resumes:

EXPERIENCED EMPLOYEE OF TWO LAW FIRMS in past summers. Have always worked despite carrying heavy academic loads.

HAVE CURRENT 3.7 GPA IN UNIVERSITY OF TEXAS HONORS PROGRAM. Plan to attend law school. Was National Merit Scholar Finalist.

CHARACTERIZED BY PAST SUPERVISORS AS ORGANIZED, hard worker, who is time-efficient, self-motivated, practical, and thrives under high pressure.

COMPUTER LITERATE (IBM and Macintosh)

Ms. Doe, could I talk with you personally about the kind of asset I could be to your team as a summer employee? I can be reached at the above numbers, or I'll give you a call in a few days.

Sincerely,

John Henry Browning
Enclosure

Chapter 11

New-Style Job-Hunt Techniques

I am convinced that most people are such poor job hunters because they never really are taught how, which is, after all, the way they learn the rules of baseball or writing proper themes. Job hunters actually expect to go out with no instruction or experience and be expert at finding employment! Is that sane or reasonable?

We consider the prospective employer to be in control, which starts us, the sellers, off feeling as if we are psychological underdogs. In addition, schools often still teach outdated, traditional, resume-oriented approaches to the job search. And we, as hunters, quickly find we would rather have the mail carrier bring a rejection letter than receive it in person! This, too, explains why many job hunters still lean on resumes and mass mailings, despite all the Labor Department statistics that tell us these are the *poorest* ways to locate work! ➤

Recognize that large corporations are continuing to downsize.

Recognize that large corporations continue to downsize; most jobs are available in companies of one hundred employees or less. These smaller companies are harder to identify than the obvious giants. Therefore, to crack this tough and elusive job market, you must think like a seeker and not an employer. You must use job-hunting techniques that are often different from what traditionalists and employers say they want you to do. ➤

If you are being laid off,
don't hesitate to ask your boss
for leads to decision makers,
telephone calls on your behalf,
letters of recommendation, or
even to circulate your resume.

If you are a good employee, but the project has ended or your company simply is eliminating your position; you should feel comfortable asking for help from every source. What better person to start with then the person who knows your work best and can sell you better than you could possibly do on your own? ➤

Accept that few job openings
are ever advertised.

It is estimated that only 15 to 20 percent of all jobs are ever advertised. Constantly remind yourself that before decision makers advertise, they usually search inside the organization, ask their present employees who they know, and talk with their friends.
➤

Learn not to take want ads

seriously.

How, according to the Department of Labor, do people find jobs? Here are the actual numbers behind the trends we've been discussing.

1% Private employment agencies

3% Public employment agencies

5% Help-wanted ads

6% School placement services

24% Direct contact with decision makers (asking someone for job)

45% Friends and relatives (I'm hearing 70%-80% in the 1990's.)

13% A combination of above or others (such as temporary work, contract, and consulting). ➤

Don't be lulled into thinking that you will be hired just because you are qualified.

Even if you have a good interview and possess all the relevant credentials, the *identification ingredient* is still the reason for hiring. People employ mirrors of themselves as much as possible. That's why the best-qualified person is not necessarily the one who is hired. ➤

Explore alternate ways to get inside a company.

Today, companies are more careful about hiring full-time employees. Instead, they are hiring more and more consultants, temporary, and contract workers. Employers, as we have seen, can then take a look at the kind of worker you'll be, how you fit in with their team, and decide if they want you full time.

In repeated studies of traditional versus street-smart job hunting techniques, the street smart—and therefore more assertive job hunters—found jobs quicker and with better salaries and positions. In a *tough* market, the time it takes to find a job will lengthen considerably, and the street-smart hunters' percentages will rise even higher.

So nontraditional job-hunting techniques repeatedly prove themselves. Using unconventional methods, you're more likely to find the job you want *with a higher starting salary in a shorter period of time.* ➤

Avoid personnel and human resource departments like the plague.

They are attempting to fill a recipe for a person described by the decision maker; the personnel department is therefore designed to screen people—mostly *out*. They seldom have the power to offer jobs. In addition, hiring itself is not logical because the decision maker hires—his clone! If you go to your benefactor/contact/friend who "clones" with you, then your friend sends you to his/her decision-maker friends who "clone" with him/her, your chances of being hired increase tremendously.

Simply dealing with personnel/human resources can undermine your self-confidence. If you're a masochist, go ahead. Remember, the best-qualified person does not necessarily get the job; you will be hired by your clone, the person who sees himself reflected, and who thinks you will fit in and be trainable his way.

If you do not think that fitting in is a major concern of decision makers, consider a recent study of executives within one hundred large corporations that showed that in a year they spent 4.6 weeks contending with personality clashes between workers!
➤

Find benefactors and network.

What does seeking out benefactors actually do? It allows you, like a detective, to build leads. One goes from friend to acquaintance to new friend, so you are not a *stranger* on whom the gate is continually closed. That name of a contact person, used when introducing yourself on the telephone, is the familiarity that gives us an ever-so-tiny edge.

Surprisingly, you will find friends and even slight acquaintances who will happily give you direct leads to decision makers. Chances are, too, that since those decision makers are their friends, you're more apt to clone with them, just as your friends do with you. ➤

Discover how to get past human resources to the supervisors of departments where you want to work.

First, thoroughly exploit your benefactor/contact/friend sources.

We must first define a good benefactor. This person should be reasonably outgoing, in your field (if that matters), older than you if possible (you aren't as apt to threaten them with your competence and quickness), and someone who is often out with people. Benefactors are found at all levels of the work force, but are often supervisors of some sort. Vendors, people at church or next door, co-workers, your hairdresser, or your college professor are all possibilities—as long as they fit the criteria of liking people, being able to talk, and are not perfectionistic and detail oriented. I had a client a few years ago who found the lead to his executive-level job through his wife's hairdresser!

Although they may be dear friends, most detail-oriented people will have a terrible time vouching for you because deep in their personality they feel so many things are wrong with them that they dread that something must be wrong with you. They are afraid (*perfectionism* and *fear* are synonyms) that you will make them look bad. If you go to one of these people to ask for help in building leads, and all they want to do is edit your resume, back out. You are not there to have your resume corrected, but in search of some real help in finding someone who knows decision makers. If they can't help you, don't waste your valuable time. ➤

Call a prospective benefactor and say, "May I come by for fifteen minutes for some advice?"

Fifteen minutes means you are aware that your benefactor is busy. (And everyone loves to give advice!)

Probably the first question your benefactor will ask is the same question you'll hear from a prospective employer, "What do you want?" Explain what you have in mind, all the time seeking advice on a broader view of your area (or the market).

If your benefactor turns out to be the perfectionist described above say something like, "Look, George, I know this isn't a perfect resume. There is no perfect resume. What I need from you is someone who can help me find a place to start to look for work."

If the first person you approach turns out to be the wrong person, you've got to learn to back out and say to yourself, "That guy dislikes people so much that he obviously goes to lunch alone—and happily. It is literally beyond his emotional capability to help me." Then move on. ➤

Consider alternate sources for
locating benefactors.

Additional sources of benefactors include professional and alumni groups. In addition, a good librarian often can point you to the particular trade journal for your field. In fact, a caring librarian can be one of your greatest assets in your job hunt!

Attend professional seminars, conventions, and special university speeches. A client of mine gained two valuable leads into the genetics engineering field simply by staying and talking with a speaker for a few minutes after his speech.

Another client, a new graduate looking for a sales trainee position, attended a sales motivational seminar, talked with the leader afterwards, and was brought to the stage and proudly displayed for two hundred sales managers to see. Within three minutes he had sixteen cards with invitations to call.

Build benefactors through
research.

You can certainly use newspapers to scan the want ads to see who is hiring. This can be useful to you for names of companies looking for employees of all kinds. Try to find the name of the supervisor of the area in which you would be employed. Most of your competition will be mailing in resumes to Personnel, and most will die in file 13 (the wastebasket). Even if the supervisor directs you back down to Personnel, you will often get an interview because the decision maker sent you. Remember, decision makers know about job openings long before Personnel, and they often fill them without the help of the Personnel Department.

Contact people you read about in the newspapers who have recently changed jobs in your field. Usually they have just been through what you are about to encounter and may be willing to share their experience, names of decision makers of a job they didn't fit, or unused leads.

Be aware that where there is change, there often is opportunity. Usually, when mergers and acquisitions take place, many employees leave, take early retirement, or simply don't fit in with the new management. Approach the decision makers of these companies, too.

Do the necessary research to develop a list of prospective employers. Spend some time learning about company executives, markets, products, and services through listings such as *Standard and Poor's Register of Corporations, Directors and Executives, The Thomas Register of American Manufacturing* and *Thomas Register File, Moody's* (lists over 20,000 corporations), Dun and Bradstreet's *The Million Dollar Directory, The National Job Bank,* and *The Career Guide.*

The Yellow Pages can educate you about who in your area is in your business. For instance, suppose you have decided what you do best is computer special projects and conversions, and you enjoy the manufacturing inventory control environment. Scan the Yellow Pages for the kinds of companies who need inventory control. List companies you think you might like to work for, and search for names of decision makers through your friends, local professional groups, trade associations, Chambers of Commerce, and the library. Then call and ask for the name of the person who heads Inventory Control. That's all you want. If the receptionist asks why, say you need the correct name and address because you must write a letter. ➤

Write notes and make initial calls to develop leads.

This is employing that twenty-four percent way to find a job (from the Department of Labor statistics).

After you have a list of companies and have verified by telephone the name, title, and address of the decision maker, then write a handwritten personal note on good quality paper (I use fold-over stationery in an ivory color). Men should use the smaller-size stationery called Monarch. In the lower left-hand corner of the envelope write *Personal and Confidential.*

In this note you tell the decision maker briefly about your experience and education, if it is relevant. Then you ask them if you could call next Tuesday (or Wednesday or Thursday) between ten and twelve "for a few minutes for some advice." Should you miss them then, you will call right after five or the next day. These are the usual times decision makers are easiest to reach.

Dear Mr. Jones:

I am a career and outplacement consultant with over ten years experience. I'm considering a change in career direction. Because I am in a position that demands most of my time, I need to talk with someone with a broader overview of the market in our area. I am not asking you for a job.

If I called you Tuesday morning between 10 and 12, could you give me just a few minutes on the phone for some advice? If we don't connect then, I'll call later in the day or later in the week.

Respectfully,

Eleanor Baldwin
214/555-2992

Schedule writing and mailing notes (as well as making telephone calls) all day every day if you do not have a job. When you are still employed and time away from your present job is very limited, write your notes on the weekend and make two or three phone calls at an early lunch hour. (Often decision makers do not return to the office until well after lunch.)

Slide past the secretary by saying, "May I speak to John Brown (Full name with no "Mr."), and would you tell him Joe/Jane Doe is calling." When you are asked what this is about say, "This is in reference to personal correspondence and he is expecting my call." If you continue to be asked, say "I know how busy your boss is, but I only need a minute to ask a quick question."

If the decision maker is out, say "I'm going to be away from my desk, can you suggest the best time to reach him?" Ask her name and note it on your portfolio; secretaries are very good allies! After several calls, you may become the best of friends. ➤

Follow this model in determining what to say once you get the decision maker on the phone.

Repeat your note briefly. Gain rapport by asking questions that demand the decision maker pay close attention. Try not to flatly state your case. For instance:

"Hello, my name is Jane Doe. Joe Smith suggested I call you as a person who could give me some advice. I've been working over ten years in sales, marketing, and operations management. Since I have been heavily involved with my present (or past position), I need to speak to someone who can give me a broader overview of the market for my speciality in this area. I am not asking you for a job."

Then you begin to ask questions, because the listener must pay attention when being asked questions.

Is my specialty and expertise in demand in this market? How do you see the long-term expectations in this field? Can you describe the best worker in this job you have ever supervised (education, salary, personality, experience)? What companies have gained new contracts? What kind of qualifications do I need to apply? What advice can you, as a decision maker, give me? What kind of salary could I expect?

Eventually, you will ask, *Would you know someone who would be interested in someone of my experience, education, and personality? Do you know anyone who may be thinking of hiring?*

Keep in mind that you want to have the decision maker do most of the talking. If you talk, he or she learns; if he or she talks, you learn.

Get to know the decision maker a little; perhaps you could call again for advice. After a few calls to decision makers, you will have begun to build a network of benefactors: people you can keep in touch with or who may actually (glory be!) call you about openings.

Again, the last thing you will say is, "Now that you have had time to know my experience, Mr./Ms. Smith, do you know of any company or person that I should contact?" Once you have one name, ask if he or she knows another. Now you are no longer a stranger, since you can call the new contacts (with permission, of course) using Mr. or Ms. Jones's name as an opener.

Sometimes the end of the day is a good time to catch executives, relaxed, sans secretary. (Remember the story of Sue, the nonprofit agency professional.) Know that these busy executives are just like the rest of us: they want you to respect their time, and they don't want to be tricked or pressured.

Recent clients have indicated that they are able to locate up to seventy-five percent of the people to whom they write notes. Remember, job hunting is a numbers game, so the more people you contact, the quicker something will happen.

Should you have the luck (and it happens) to find there is a job opening coming up, say: "How exciting; this is wonderful! Could I stop by tomorrow (or Wednesday after work) at eight or eleven? Which time would be more convenient?"

If they ask you to send your resume, tell them you will be on their side of town tomorrow and will bring it in person.

If there is no opening right now (more likely) say, "May I come by to speak with you for a few minutes to thank you in person. I want you to remember me should something open up in the future." If not, leave your telephone number anyway, just in case they change their mind and think of someone who can help you. Write a thank you for the time they spent with you, too.

Understand that your goal is to get the decision maker on the phone.

Understand that your goal is getting the decision maker on the phone instead of getting an appointment; don't ask the secretary to have him or her return your call. Protect the secretary's position by saying, after the first call, "I'm going to be out the rest of the day and thought I'd try to catch [the decision maker] before I leave." If you make it clear that you are unreachable for a day or two, you won't leave the burden of contact on the decision maker. This gives you a chance to build rapport with the secretary, too. Know that you will probably call many times before you finally reach the decision maker. ➤

Use informational interviewing
only sparingly.

This is another tactic, but it is often overused today. If you want to ask questions about the company, I recommend contacting Personnel Departments, especially when you have no place else to start. Say, "I'm new in town, (or "so glad to be back home"), and I have decided to call three firms to find out about the current job market. Can you give me fifteen minutes for some advice?" ➤

Make personal contacts instead
of mailing resumes.

Don't waste precious time writing, rewriting, and mailing resumes, instead of interviewing. Jobs are often made for people who impress the boss. But, in order to impress the boss, you will need to see the boss in person. ➤

Consciously add to and always

maintain your contacts with

neighbors, friends, association

members, acquaintances, and

past co-workers.

When we passed from the Industrial Age to the Information Age, we also passed from the hierarchical world into the networking world.

You *never* have to stop networking—not even after you find the job of your dreams. All you need to do is adjust the *way* you network. ➤

Plan on making many calls and having many personal interviews.

Turnover in the past has run from 10 to 25 percent annually, though it is even higher in the quicksand of today's job market. You should try to arrange over ten interviews for job openings in order to obtain as many offers as possible. You may have to make dozens of telephone calls and write lots of notes and letters to make this happen. But remember, *you* are in control, and locating a job on your own is a wonderful confidence builder! ➤

Keep foremost in your mind when

approaching a prospective

employer that it is what you

can do to help his or her

company make or save money that

will make you an attractive

candidate.

We have long lived in a competitive capitalistic economy, and the rest of the world seems to be rapidly joining us. Businesses that do not make a profit simply cannot stay in business. If you are interviewing with an institution or the government, you need to look like someone who can solve problems. All you are to an employer is *help in making revenue or in problem solving*. Therefore, you should delay discussing any of your own needs, except in passing, until you have convinced the interviewers that you can become the help *they* need. ➤

Realize job hunting is sales and that you can learn to sell yourself.

Know that you are playing a numbers game. You must sell yourself as literally as you would sell a car or refrigerator. The odds—especially in a tough market—strongly suggest that you will hear your share of nos, but there will be an occasional yes, too. You will need only one job at a time!

Let me tell you about one of my most resounding no's. I had an early Monday appointment with the president of a company to discuss outplacement (a nice term for teaching people who are being let go how to hunt for new jobs) for a department of his firm. I had talked him into the meeting on the telephone. On arrival, I found myself going up in the elevator with the person I was to see. I knew there was no rapport between us, because I'm serious and very caring of people who are being let go. I gave it my best, however, and when the rejection came, I backed out, and didn't take it personally. I thought of myself as a brown refrigerator caught in a blue kitchen. It just wasn't a good match.

Selling yourself means not taking such situations personally. Every rejection you experience is only one "no" on the way to a "yes." ➤

Research leads.

Research leads to companies through your local library business reference section, your benefactors, and the company's competitors. A stock broker or large library will have stock buyers' guides such as *Standard & Poors* and *Moody's*. You can search these guides for companies that interest you and contact the person listed as their Investor Relations Representative.

One woman who wanted an entry-level position in a genetics engineering firm found after research that the largest companies seemed to be grouped in two areas around San Diego and San Francisco. She lived far from those cities and had very little cash after working her way through college. So she used the investor relations contacts provided on the *Standard & Poors* sheets. To save money, she called after 5pm (which was 3pm in California). The person listed was invariably no longer in that position (common in a new industry with heavy research and development).

Her conversations went like this:

"This is Maria Adams in Chicago. Is John Brown (the Stockholder Relations person) in?"

"No, Mr. Brown is no longer with us."

"Oh, really, then who has taken John's place?"

Then she would talk with the *new* Stockholder Relations person and say:

"I understand you've taken John's place. This is Maria Adams in Chicago, and I'm calling to learn about your company."

Remember that the Stockholder Relations person's job is to make it easy for people to invest in his or her company. Maria would build rapport and soon have the name of the decision maker in the company department in which she wanted to work.

Maria ended up mailing twelve cover letters with resumes—after many telephone calls, since she obviously could not deliver them in person. These were sent to the people she had talked to on the telephone, and they hand carried them to the decision makers in her area of expertise.

She carefully saved her money for a spring trip to interview. She received six interview invitations and three job offers! Those are astoundingly good statistics. (By the way, Maria had a very strange degree—a mixture of genetics and communication. What's more, she was older than the usual college graduate. Had she gone to Personnel she would have fit *no* job description they had ever heard and would have been considered unemployable!)

But since she had a goal, Maria is now making somewhere in the seventy-five thousand dollar range; not bad for a young woman who could barely afford a long-distance phone call six years earlier.

If you can locate it, another help is the simply and clearly written book *The Best Way in the World for a Woman to Make Money*. The authors provide scripts of techniques for getting past "the guardians of the gate"—secretaries or receptionists. I recommend this hard-to-find book to *both* sexes as not only a sales method text, but also as a way to see how your field stacks up against others. You'll find that it is often *where* (what industry and position) you are and not *now good* you are that determines how much money you make. ➤

Accept that you must toil many hours weekly to locate the kind of position you want.

If you are out of work, finding new employment should be your forty-hour weekly job. You will need a written daily plan for calls, notes, and interviews. Mark off items as you complete them. This will help to give your psyche the needed boost to continue until success is yours.

If you are still employed and looking for a new job, make job-hunting work your intense avocation for a few months. ➤

Organize to find a good job.

Organization is the key to locating a career position. For those of you who think quickly (who finish other people's sentences, go down the hall and forget why, wiggle when you have to sit very long, or wait until the last minute to do things) organization is often a real problem. This type of person interrupts himself with another idea or rabbit to chase, gets bored easily, and is prone to follow up poorly, if at all.

And then there are those people who have all the qualities to be well organized, but find every excuse not to get started (a fearful perfectionistic trait, usually). An example that comes quickly to mind is a building manager client that I met at a local restaurant one evening. I asked her how the job hunt was progressing. She said she had not been able to get started because this week was her boyfriend's birthday! She obviously was finding reason after reason not to begin to hunt. You have to slide off that chair and go out and do it. The trick to getting the right job is simply staying in there—and staying and staying. ➤

Be prepared to make mistakes.

Know that it's necessary to get out and fall on your face a few times, because you're not going to do everything well at first. The only difference between a successful person and a failure is the number of times the success gets up and learns from his or her mistakes.

In a Steve Klein seminar here in Dallas I remember his explaining that goal setters will accomplish on average a little over a third of their goals. His suggestion was to have many goals so you will, logically, accomplish quite a lot anyway. However, if you accomplish one-third, that means you will still *not* accomplish two-thirds! You could, if you are a scared job hunter, classify those two-thirds of your goals as "failures." I prefer to call them slogging through the necessary mud in order to accomplish the one-third! ➤

Pretend you're Sherlock Holmes

Finding a job is like solving a mystery. You'll encounter many dead ends but eventually, if the numbers are great enough, you will locate a job. That doesn't mean, particularly for the detail-oriented person, that paranoia and insecurity will not be your constant companion. Job hunting is stressful, and even *knowing* that you will hear no more often than yes, you may still find that you feel rejected. Now is the time to remember the sales rule of Twenty-One. Reduced to essentials this means you must make twenty-one sales (job) calls in order to make one sale (get a job). Are you willing to make twenty-one employment (sales) calls in order to get a job? Or are you going to hide out at home and mail resumes to ads, call personnel agencies, and try to let George do it?

You are George! ➤

Be realistic about the time it takes to find a job.

I have seen people in deep, dark depression after two weeks and three interviews with no job. It takes an average of three *months* to find a decent job early in your career. As you climb higher, that time lengthens, because there are always fewer jobs at higher levels. In a tough market, it could be even longer. Executives are often out of full-time work for over a year.

Keep things in perspective. ➤

Do the impossible: find time to hunt for a job when you already have one.

When your present job is taking all your time, how can you possibly find time to look? You know that looking while you are still employed is the strongest position for you. The same psychology is at work as when the girl who already has a date to the prom is attractive to others because somebody else wants her!

You will find time and energy by being organized. For most of us, it has been easy to organize the employer's tasks at work rather than our own. There is that imposed schedule. Now is the time, however, to put *yourself* first for a change. So, on your daily calendar, you will schedule making two or three phone calls a day, during an early lunch if necessary. With your yellow pad that fits into your nice portfolio at the ready, document each call and every note or letter you mail or carry to someone for later follow up. ➤

New Way #161

Break the job hunt into simple chores.

Break the job hunt into little doable chores so it isn't a great horrible pain. A great horrible pain (for most of us, anyway) is the whole experience of being fired or being out of work for a long time (particularly for males who are raised to *be* their job). Take it a step at a time. ➤

New Way #162

Appeal to your prospective employer's sense of fairness in managing scheduling conflicts.

A relative of mine handled this well by saying to a prospective employer, "I know that you want me to be as conscientious with you as I am with my present employer. Because of that, the only time I can fly up to interview will be weekends." They agreed on a Saturday, complete with psychological testing, and he was hired!

Negotiate for interview times after five, on holidays, or weekends. You'll be surprised at what you hear in response. ➤

Follow up and stay up.

How do you keep from going bonkers while waiting to hear about a call or interview? Plan each day so that you keep on doing things toward another position. Never take *any* promise for granted. Then, despite yesterday's setback (or indeterminate nothingness—no results), you can learn to feel success daily because you've completed everything on your daily list and made more telephone calls. Exercise often and keep happy people around you. Keep looking ahead. ➤

Make it incredibly easy for
people to get in touch with you.

A decision maker needs to find you rapidly for interviewing or other questions. I find some of my clients *still* view answering machines negatively. But the machine is the most logical way to handle this problem of availability, especially if you travel or are out of your office constantly. Perhaps you'd rather have your calls forwarded to someone who is always there.

If you decide on my choice, the answering machine, make your answering tape a professional communications tool. My weekend and evening business tape says in a very happy voice, "This is Eleanor Baldwin, Ltd., and Hour Savers Career Services twenty-four-hour line. We want to answer your questions and return your calls. After the tone, if you will leave your message with name, number, and time, someone will return your call as quickly as possible. Thank you for calling. Good-bye."

- Make your message warm, not cute. Save the impressionists and background music for later when only your friends will be calling. Make sure to ask for call time, telephone number, and message.

- Call your tape your "hot-line" or "call-in center offering twenty-four-hour coverage." ■

Chapter 12

Interviewing and Nonverbal Communication

Mean Business

"You may be surprised, Eleanor, but I didn't hire the person with the best qualifications!" Since it didn't surprise me a bit, knowing that decision makers hire their clones, I asked my lunch companion what made him decide to hire that particular person. "Well," he said, "She looked good, she gave me the feeling that she could learn, and I thought she'd fit in with the rest of my staff."

And, of course, he was right.

Then I asked why he didn't hire the best-qualified person. "Well," he said, "Her hair looked oily and she never smiled. I got the impression that although she could do the job starting tomorrow, she was a loner who would not become a vital part of my team." ➤

Interviewing is theater; plan accordingly.

The principal reason people are initially considered for a job are

1. how they look

2. first impression of speech and body language

So it is vital that you be appropriately dressed for your job and locality or you won't get past the first thirty seconds (the "thirty-second barrier") of the interview. Neatness counts! A whole lot!

For years now I have asked decision makers in my seminars this question:

"How long after the job prospect walks in the door does it take you to decide whether you are going to talk with that candidate seriously about your opening or not."

The answers ranged from *immediately* to *by the time they sit down*. Obviously, then, a neat, smilingly confident image will pay off in short order. And, unfair as it may appear, first impressions are *almost* everything. ➤

Be prepared to look square.

This is especially true if you have a position where you might handle money! White-collar men should wear conservative suits, unless this is inappropriate for your locale or trade. It is a compliment to most prospective employers to be overdressed a little rather than underdressed for an interview. It indicates how seriously you view interviewing with this person. Wear long-sleeved, white or pale blue shirts and silk ties with small patterns. Absolutely no bow ties. Avoid strong shaving lotion. ➤

If you are a man, get a haircut; men who wear short hair fare best in interviews.

Facial hair is acceptable only in a very few positions (such as psychologist or college professor). For most men, beards are just one more difficulty to get past when interviewing for business positions. Bearded men have a nonconformist image.

I have warned several of my clients about inappropriate (for their profession) beards, and almost to a man they have had trouble finding work until after they shaved.

In addition, make sure your shoes are shined and do not wear more than a watch and wedding ring as jewelry. Be clean and absolutely neat. ➤

Learn how to dress as a

businesswoman.

White-collar women, because we have so many choices, tend to make multiple mistakes. Always wear a suit (or skirt and dress) with jacket. Jackets mean clout for women. Without a jacket, you are likely to be asked very quickly your typing speed!

Your outfit should be a navy or a similar medium to dark color worn with a conservative white or pastel blouse, unless you are in a fashion-forward field or live in a very laid back locale.

Leave your purse at home; purses say "Mom." Always carry a briefcase; I think the sachel type is easiest to handle in an interview situation since it isn't so bulky. Then slip your attractive portfolio (leather folder with tablet on the right side and a place for your resumes and reference sheets on the left) in one side, leaving room for your billfold, car keys, and so forth, in the middle. Like your jacket, the briefcase means clout. ➤

Doublecheck feminine grooming
before interviewing.

With your interview outfit ready, now check personal appearance. Lots of obvious points here: jewelry, hair, nails, excessive makeup, perfume, and short skirts are forbidden, even if they are the fashion. Make sure everything about your makeup, hair, and clothes is subtle and controlled. You can be wild and crazy after work! Remember, this is theater; you need to dress for your role. ➤

Triplecheck neatness if you are a service or blue-collar man or woman.

You need to look your best and very neatest, too. And this is most often the kind of individual who may declare his independence from conformity by looking absolutely awful! You probably can find more bad grooming on engineering and construction projects than anywhere else. What those workers don't seem to realize is that short hair and good grooming pays off in promotions and dollars. Management judges you not simply by how you perform your job, but again, by how well you look the part.

Well cared for shirts and skirts or slacks are good. The service industry is so broad that casual or more formal clothing may be acceptable. If you are required to take some kind of test that requires physical effort (as welders are), be prepared to take it in proper attire—neat, clean, and polished.

Body Language
Statistics have shown that even in the logical and analytical field of engineering, only 15 percent of getting that job is qualifications! A person's tone of voice, posture, facial expression, and eye contact all give clues about his or her feelings and attitudes. Be sensitive to these in yourself and others. Don't fidget or slouch. Face the interviewer in a relaxed, open manner. Never, but never, cross your arms—this is one of the most negative of all body language moves! ➤

Be mindful that from sixty-five to eighty-five percent of finding employment is nonverbal.

Unconscious judgments are made of personal appearance and use of body language. You need to be aware of how you are selling yourself. Enhance your credibility by doing the following things:

- **Smile.** Smiling can erase things you say in an interview that turn out to be less than intelligent. I teach my clients to smile often. People who smile simply look pleasant to be around. I write "lighten up," which makes me smile, on my own interview portfolio.

- **Maintain good eye contact.** This says you are sincere and self-confident.

- **Speak** in a firm, confident, and not-too-loud voice that is not too quiet or too shaky. Gain rapport through small talk before talking about really important things. Say, "Can you take time to talk with me now?" "Could you give me a few minutes for some advice?"

- **Enter the room** with a firm handshake, a pleasant smile, and good eye contact. Reach for your portfolio and say, "May I take a few notes? I don't want to miss anything." Hitch the chair closer to the desk or balance the portfolio (which contains your information sheet) on your knee. What this does is make you lean forward, and leaning forward and nodding when people talk is body language that shows acceptance of the speaker. The portfolio also allows you to have written cues to proper body language on your information sheet. Holding the portfolio and pen will also keep you from doing strange things with your hands, such as tapping, crossing your arms, or feeling as if you have three extra hands!

- **Listen!** Don't look and sound like a trapped animal that must babble on due to something akin to dementia.

- **Maintain good posture.** Mirror the interviewer's physical posture and breathing; this says, "You and I are much alike." Do not cross your arms or legs or suddenly lean away from the interviewer. That is body language that says you have become closed or self-protective. (Have you ever noticed two or three men talking in the hall at work with their arms crossed—a very defensive posture most often noted in technical environments?) Maintain simple, straight posture to appear open and sincere. You should never cross your arms unless you're freezing to death!

- **Maintain enough distance.** Americans like you best at arm's length. ➤

Develop protective interview techniques.

Learn to develop some protective interviewing techniques to deal with "Sherman Tanks"—intimidating decision makers.

1. When someone is doing a power job on you, just remember that you can only accommodate one emotion at a time. I pretend to be my heroine, Venita Van Caspel, and respond cool and professionally as I think she would (and believe me, I am no actress). I don't stay awed long, because my heroine wouldn't.

2. Try one of the old cliches: visualize them in huge boxer shorts decorated with hearts and flowers.

3. We are all equal under God's eyes; you cannot win *everyone* over, at least not if you have any convictions of your own. ➤

Before the interview, decide what you will do if the interviewer is rude, flaky, or scares you.

If staying cool doesn't work, simply understand that the problem is the interviewer's and you should feel sorry for him or her. Remember that *you* are in control, not the interviewer. ➤

Understand that it may not be possible to win over an interviewer who doesn't like you.

But you can try. Some interviewers get off on the wrong foot, too. Try to stick in long enough to understand the intention, or perhaps *your* prejudices are getting in the way.

However, it has been my experience that some persuasive sales-type personalities stick in too long trying to change an antagonistic prospective employer's attitude. That time could probably be much better spent looking elsewhere. If the cloning isn't there, often it never will be. ➤

Know that your interviewer
isn't having any fun, either.

So you hate interviewing! Understand, then, that interviewing for most decision makers is probably ninety-nine on *their* list of one hundred fun things for the day, too.

We're talking about the boss who is not a professional interviewer (as are those in Human Resources/Personnel). So the decision makers you talk with probably won't be too slick, and if you understand the psychology of the interview, you can often give it direction. ➤

Clue into what employers say
they are looking for.

When interviewed about hiring, decision makers say they are seeking younger workers with maturity, education, a good personal appearance, good communication ability, and a winning personality. At executive levels individual growth potential and creativity are more important than specific industry or business background, according to a recruiting firm study. But I have found in today's buyer's market for mid- to upper-level jobs, decision makers are very picky about specific experience, too.

Every employer is different. Be on the lookout for the (often subtle) indications that will tell you what your interviewer wants.
➤

Plan your pre-interview
strategy.

Research the company, remembering that knowledge is power. (This bears repeating because it is so universally ignored.) It is amazing to me that people will actually go to interviews without knowing what the company does! Not knowing about the organization you want to work for is a common mistake. Try to find out the products or services, history, business methods, and organizational structure, locations, reputation, philosophy, industry standing, and prospects for growth of any company with which you have an interview. Look in

- Annual reports, catalogs, press releases, and other company literature

- *The New York Times* index, *Business Periodicals* index, and *College Placement Annual*

- Business directories, trade associations and professional society publications, almanacs, yearbooks, magazines, newsletters, and computer databases

Research the decision maker through your benefactor or an inside contact to find common interests, likes and dislikes, college, major, friends, hobbies. It's less important to fill the recipe of qualifications they have given Personnel/Human Resources, than it is to have common background or interests.

Often the decision maker's secretary is someone who will help. Tell the secretary or receptionist that you have an interview and in order to be prepared so you won't take too much time, could she/he describe the decision maker's interests and personality. You can ask questions about where he/she worked before, where he moved from, went to college, etc. ➤

Arrive five to ten minutes

early for any interview.

This will allow time for parking and traffic problems, a quick visit to the restroom, and a few minutes getting lost in the parking garage (surely someone besides me does this).

You can quietly ask the receptionist polite questions, scan materials about the company, and go over the notes you have made so names and information will be fresh in your mind. Look like a calm and collected professional.

When you arrive too early, you put pressure on the interviewer. Should he/she keep you waiting a long time, however, you have a psychological advantage if you have shown up a few minutes ahead of time. ➤

Try to stall when asked to fill out employment applications before the interview.

Say, "Thank you, I'll do this later when I can be very neat and sure of dates and so on; then I'll return it to you." Remember, these forms are screening devices.

Or you could say, "I'm not sure this is really a job interview, so I would like this information to be confidential unless a real position is discussed. Then I'll return it completed with exact dates." ➤

Manage the first thirty seconds with the interviewer by understanding how to step in the door.

Smile and grip the interviewer's hand securely: you know the stories about limp fish handshakes.

A strong handshake (but not too strong) communicates a body language message of proficiency, self-confidence, and a reasonably outgoing personality. You know how important first impressions are, and this is your first chance to let your body language speak for your interpersonal skills. ➤

Minimize negative body language.

Eliminate several latent body language snares by taking your attractive leather or leatherette portfolio (which holds your tablet notes, resumes, and questions about the job and the organizations you've gleaned from your own research). Smile and ask, "Mr./Ms. Jones, would you mind if I take a few notes? I don't want to forget anything."

Some initial questions that you might jot down for use are:

1. What are the most important skills for this job?

2. What are the job responsibilities?

3. How would my performance be evaluated?

4. How would I be supervised?

5. What advancement opportunities are there?

6. How much travel is required?

7. What is the last person who had this job doing? Where is he/she now?

8. Can I expect training to be provided?

9. What are the company's goals?

10. What is the company's history?

11. What is the management style of the company? ➤

Display confidence won through
thorough preparation.

It can't be overstated: your ego will be strengthened through preparation. Don't think self-confidence is being overbearing. Quiet, happy self-confidence is a way of saying that you are serious about your career and job, are eager to learn, and will be good at it. ➤

Never volunteer negative information about yourself, or let any negative or no statement stand alone without an immediate follow-up.

Remember, the interviewer is not your priest or psychiatrist!

Having to truthfully answer no to questions of education and experience, however, can be dealt with by instantly saying something to answer objections, as salespeople are taught to do. For instance, should you be asked if you have an MBA and you must answer no, then without delay (or even taking a deep breath), tell about the relevant seminars and training sessions you've attended. If possible, drop a few well-known motivational trainers/speakers names for snob appeal.

Suppose you have to endure what many do today in our economic downturns. You have had several jobs in the last few years, not because you were incompetent, but because your employers went out of business or trimmed staff to the bone. Then a question of why you've had so many jobs can be met with "You know what the Texas (or New York or Boston) economy is like." ➤

Rejoice: it is not necessarily the best-qualified people who are hired.

The people who get hired are often the people who mirror the interviewer, smile, look like they will fit in with the others, appear to be trainable the boss's way, and perhaps possess other illogical qualifications that have nothing to do with education or experience. All you need is for that person to be you, once, in the right setting.

For instance, James, a former client, was describing his hiring of a new second-in-command. I asked what he was looking for, and his reply was, "Someone who can stand up to my Sherman Tank boss, but who doesn't want to take my job!"

Have you ever been depressed because you had all the qualifications for a job but weren't hired? Maybe you didn't look like you could handle Sherman Tanks! ➤

Pretend you are an inanimate
object to protect your ego.

We must shield our self-confidence. One way that I found to do this was to pretend that I was a large, brown refrigerator, so that when I ventured out to interview in what turned out be a blue kitchen where my brown refrigerator didn't fit, I did not internalize the rejection as my failure, but I considered it to be the failure of *the match*!

In other words, if the rapport isn't there, you must learn to say to yourself, "Too bad that person doesn't know a good potential employee when he sees one! I really wasted my time with him/her" (and the blue kitchen). ➤

Do not internalize tough
interview questions as failure
on your part.

Confrontation is sometimes used as a trial of your composure by a few intimidating decision makers to see how you'll react. Other difficult or strange interviewers use silence as a power stance. Don't fall apart. Use your information sheet to start asking questions yourself. Qualify those strange, vaguely threatening queries.

Think about it: unless you've hooked up with a truly maniacal interviewer, what's being tested is your ability to handle pressure. Keep your cool. ➤

Know that good employment-seeking techniques are always more important than specific experience or fine credentials.

As we have seen, interviewing well is so much more important than your experience, a great resume, or marvelous credentials, so use your resume as a support to your professionalism, not the major tactic in your fight in a tough job market.

Several years ago I read of a personable, college-educated professional who, as a rather unusual hobby, interviewed for over three hundred jobs in broadly diverse fields over a seven-year period. Many of these jobs he was obviously unqualified to do.

He received approximately two hundred job offers. Obviously, his personality impressed a good many people! ➤

Stay positive; avoid

criticizing.

Don't criticize your present employer or team members or, worst of all, any geographical location—especially if that's where you're looking for a job. This could be the decision markers hometown and most of us are quite chauvinistic about home. ➤

Note these areas you can discuss to help gain rapport with the interviewer.

1. "I understand you went to the University of Miami. So did my brother."

2. "Our friend, James, says your hobby is painting. Do you do oils or water colors?"

3. "I understand you moved here from Montana. Where did you live there?"

4. "Why did *you* decide to go with this company?"

5. "Who was, in your opinion, the best person who ever held this position? What did he/she do that makes you remember him/her so favorably? ➤

List these more serious questions on your information sheet.

1. "What is a quick job description of your opening, and what kind of person do you think would be the best fit?"

2. "Where is the person who had this job before?"

3. "Could I meet the team I'd work with and be shown through the offices?"

4. "Would you show me where I'd fit into the organization as a whole?"

5. Who are your major competitors? What do you think makes you different?"

6. "What challenges are both your group and the company currently facing? ➤

Be prepared to respond to "Tell me about yourself."

Over sixty percent of interviews begin with "Tell me about yourself." Most of us take this demand literally and project on to the interviewer what we think he/she wants to hear. However, usually the decision maker says this phrase just to have a place to get started. This is where a sales technique called *qualifying* or *probing* can save you from yourself.

Asking questions to find and fill needs is what qualifying really means. If you were selling me a refrigerator, you would ask what size and color refrigerator I want, whether I need a top or bottom freezer, ice maker, from which side the door needs to open—but if you walk into a job interview and someone says "Tell me about yourself," we literally try to! We forget, because we fail to transfer sales qualifying to the personal level.

Let me recount how *not* to respond to "Tell me about yourself." When I lived in New Orleans, I bombed on this front twice in one week. In the first instance, I knew what this employer's problem was and when he said "Tell me about yourself," I tried to solve his problem my way. Instead, in his mind, I became the person he'd just fired! After being stalled at the one-minute barrier a second time (I was older, taller, quicker, and more intense than the male interviewer), I knew there was something I was doing wrong.

Finally, I realized I wasn't qualifying my sales. Below is the qualifying response that I worked out and memorized to tell clients.

"Mr. Lawry, if you can give me some idea—perhaps from my resume or what you know of your needs—then I'll be able to bring up from my background things most *helpful* to you. I know how busy you are, and I don't want to waste your time." (Then pause, smile, and wait. Let the silence deepen.)

Salespeople call qualifying "answering a question with a question." Qualify or probe to fill the interviewer's needs: you've got to become the help they're seeking. ➤

Do this if you're asked a negative question like "What's your greatest weakness?"

This is the second most asked question. And how do you respond to a negative of this kind? I use the first-I'll-tell-you-the-good-news-and-then-the-bad-news technique! This requires that you be able to discuss yourself, your assets, and your deficits readily.

Using this system, when posed with "What's your greatest weakness" I would say:

> "Mr./Ms. Smith, I'm the kind of results-oriented person who likes to get things done, and because of that, my weakness is probably impatience with circumstances and people who do not respond quickly. I'm working on that."

Or, for a finance/accounting person:

> "Ms. Jones, I'm a detailed and analytical personality whose day is made when everything balances, although my weakness is that in that enjoyment, I sometimes lose track of the bigger picture. I'm working on that."

For a sales representative:

> "Mr. Black, because I'm a successful cold caller whose day is made when I make a good sale, like most sales personalities probably my weakness is not liking paperwork. I've worked on organizing to make reporting quicker and painless." ➤

Turn around the interviewer's objections. Never let a negative statement stand without a rebuttal.

What could some of these objections be? Well, almost anything, but these are common:

"You seem to have changed jobs a lot" or "Your career seems to have no focus or direction."

Answer: "You know what the job market in this area has been the past few years. I, too, am looking for some stability."

or

Answer: "While I am young, I decided to try several different directions in order to find my niche. I've discovered what it is now."

"You seem never to have changed jobs."

Answer: "If you'll examine my resume, you'll see the rapid progression and flexible experience that I gained where I was."

or

Answer: "We lived in an area of high unemployment (or low opportunity). I was fortunate to be employed at all."

or

Answer: "I found the work I did fascinating and a continual learning experience."

"You don't have the proper education."

Answer: "Statistically, only two-thirds of workers actually are employed in their degree areas. The hands-on experience and continuing education I've gained prove that I am competent in this area."

"You're overqualified and would get bored quickly."

Answer: "I'm trying to downsize the demands of work, and am seeking work with fewer challenges. If you are worried about salary, I'm sure we can work something out."

"You have no background in our industry."

Answer: "Some employers have seen my flexibility and creativity as a real asset to pump new blood into their systems. As you'll note on my resume, I've used the same talents and expertise and applied it to various problems. I've been cited as a problem solver who can think." ➤

Use psychology to answer

"What's your best asset?"

Your best asset is whatever the interviewers need.

There is little point in initially talking about something in your background they *don't* need. That is why you qualify them by asking questions to find and fill specific needs. You simply are not there long enough for them to know your heart. So what you say must matter to them—quickly! ➤

Handle felt but unasked objections just as you would an articulated objection.

If you really feel you are in danger of being removed from consideration because of one of those under-the-table considerations—your age, sex, race, or level of experience—handle those problems up front.

A method I've used personally is to say to the interviewer, "I know *you* are not the kind of person who would be prejudiced against (a woman)(someone who's worked many years)(someone with experience in another field)(an ethnic)(someone older than you). . . because I feel that you are a bottom-liner who considers employees by whether they can do the job and do it well."

This usually defuses "good ol' boys," opinionated interviewers and brash young managers very quickly. No one wants to consider himself prejudiced (despite the fact that we *all* are to some degree). ➤

Try these answers for "What are your career goals?" "Where do you want to be in two (five, ten) years?"

1. Balance ambition ("my ultimate goal is executive management") with filling their need for now ("but right now I want to be the best trainee you've ever had in this department").

2. If you are older or undecided, you could say: "In this convulsive economy who is to say exactly where we rise. I have done well in all my jobs, and being productive is what gives me the greatest satisfaction."

3. If you honestly don't know what you want, consider saying, "This is such a changing world that I've decided my option for now is going to be flexibility. I really need a little more time in the work world to be knowledgeable enough to know my track." ➤

Know yourself well enough to provide a compelling answer to: "What would be your perfect job?"

Obviously you should tailor your answer to the situation, but you must know yourself well to answer this.

I myself would say in answer to this question, "One where I can take my experience to have control of a specific area so my results-orientation, creative problem-solving, and self-motivation are assets to the team. One where there is some high-profile exposure as well as the opportunity to be paid well for what I produce." ➤

Respond this way to "What do you know about our company?" or "What can you do for us?"

I will assume you would not dare go to an interview without knowing about the company and having notes about the organization jotted on your information sheet. In answer to "What can you do for us," simply state, "I can help you make or save money," and be ready to tell exactly how. ➤

"Why did you choose this career?"

Answer this question by reciting the natural aptitudes and talents that led you in this employment direction. ➤

Consider these responses to "Why have you had so many (or so few) jobs?"

If you've had many jobs (one every year or so for the past few years), you can say:

1. "You know the kind of market we've been in. There were two layoffs, and one company I worked for is no longer in business."

2. "I've been hired away," or "I've changed to gain broader experience."

3. "While I'm young, I want to find out what's out there and what I want to be my life's work."

If you have had very few, you can call attention to the progression through job titles within a single company. ➤

Be ready to talk about the achievements that gave you the most satisfaction.

But make sure they are relevant to what the interviewers seem to need. *Don't* babble on endlessly about things that satisfied you but have nothing to do with the prospective employer's business.

➤

Circumvent questions like "Will you relocate?"

Say that relocation is negotiable, given the proper incentive un-less relocation is *absolutely* out for you and your family. Even in that case, you are probably best advised to "finesse" this issue.

➤

New Way #203

Provide strong responses to questions about why you want the job.

Cite past experience and talent in the field; how the position is a step up in influence or title; the company stronger; or how the opportunity to advance greater. ➤

New Way #204

Answer "Why did you leave your last job?" this way.

If the reason was simply dissatisfaction, usually with a person, do not criticize. I have had clients who said nicely, "My very competent boss is not much older than I am. Although I hate to leave, I must move on in order to move up."

Or you might try, "The duties of my present job are no longer the track on which I want my career to travel." ➤

Be prepared to work around what you consider really difficult questions.

If you were fired, try these:

1. "With the reorganization at ABC, the new management felt I, along with many others, were identified with the former management and no longer fit their corporate mold."

2. "The new manager brought in people with whom she'd worked in the past."

3. "The company had begun to cut back."

If you are older, try:

"Mr. Jones, I know you are the kind of person who puts value on the lessons learned through experience. We learn to work flexibly with all types and ages of people, or people my age have already opted out of the system. Actually, I am much quicker to respond now than when younger, because I usually know where and how I can quickly get something done. Younger people often seem to be restless and looking for green pastures. I'm steady and loyal. That translates into solid production and cost savings for you."

Confidential responses to a recent survey of forty top-level decision makers found that, in general, older employees were considered the best workers, except in high tech. Words often used to describe their group were "loyal," "stable lifestyle," "hard workers," "owe something to job," "give 100%," "do what needs to be to be done," "dedicated," "better work habits," "conscientious," "productive," "realistic," "willing to work," and "assume it takes that."

One of my clients, aged sixty, was recently in his third and final interview for a wonderful job. The interviewer asked, "How old are you, John?" Having talked with this person many times and built rapport, John smilingly replied, "You can't ask me that." (It *is* illegal.) The interviewer said, "I just did." John, who is very quick, then responded with, "What you really want to know is how long I'll be here. I'll be here as long as you are!" He got the job.

Health is a subject that makes interviewers very nervous! Employers are very leery of hiring people who have had health, alcohol, or mental problems. If you have a back problem (who doesn't) but still function, are an on-the-wagon alcoholic, or have been in a mental institution, don't talk about it unless cornered. Then, if necessary, give proof that you are okay by showing doctor's releases or recent letters of recommendation.

If you are older and the decision maker worries about paying more for your insurance, tell him/her that, according to statistics, older workers are the healthiest workers—or they would have already opted out of the work force. ➤

Close the sale when ending the interview.

If you want the job, you can say, "What more could I do to qualify for this job?" This infers that you 1) want the job, 2) will change yourself to get it, and 3) will do it their way.

You *must* close or people will not know whether you are interested or not. I've sent people to personal contacts, and these decision makers sometimes call later and say, "Eleanor, I couldn't tell whether she wanted the job or not."

Here is what you should do to close:

Shake the interviewer's hand and ask when the final decision will be made. If the interviewer indicates no interest in hiring you, try your best to use this as a contact for further leads. If you feel some happy rapport with this interviewer, ask if you can keep in touch. (Sometimes you may call at just the right time.) ➤

Ask yourself these questions immediately after the interview.

1. Do I understand what the job entails?
2. Is the commute going to be a major difficulty?
3. Does my personality fit with the company?
4. Does this position fit with my goals?
5. If this leads to moving, will the salary make up for any changes in my cost of living? ➤

Understand that three interviews are usual in a corporate setting.

The people involved are usually the decision maker, his/her boss, and the Personnel/Human Resources people.

I was recently a member of the selection committee for a music director at a large church. We committee members collectively interviewed everyone, which has got to be a tough situation for the applicants. How on earth do you satisfy ten people at the same time?

Looking back from the job seeker's viewpoint, however, the same ingredients were at work with ten interviewers as with one: build rapport with the most powerful members, be enthusiastic, and stay relaxed and share information. Our finalists, both from Florida, were strong in all three areas, and had good (but not always the best) credentials. But most important of all, they had wonderful interpersonal skills. ➤

Try these ideas for handling
rude or sexually suggestive
interviewers.

Every now and then you will come across someone who is rude or sexually suggestive during the interview. Should this happen to you, thank them for their time and leave without making a fuss. (You don't want to earn an unjustified reputation for being "difficult.") Why bother to waste *your* valuable time on so unprofessional a person?

One of my clients, after a hard month of job hunting, decided that bosses like men to be married with three kids so they'll be steady, and women to be divorced with no prospects so they'll have to work long and hard! ➤

Stand out from the crowd: make the most of weekends.

As we've noted, you might say, "I know that you want me to be fair with you and I must be conscientious with my present employer, also. Because of that, the only time that I could really interview would be weekends."

This will not only show how conscientious you are, but give you the chance to portray your strengths in a special setting. Several years ago, my own husband was interviewed by several people, tested by a battery of psychologists, and hired—all on a single Saturday. ∎

Chapter 13

Build Self-Confidence and Follow-Up

Finding the right job means more than just "doing the right thing." It means sticking to your task and keeping your self-confidence up.

In this chapter, we'll look at some intriguing ideas for managing this essential part of your search. ➤

Realize that job hunting is an
ego-wrenching experience.

Don't expect things to be easy. Like it or not, we are going to put pressure on ourselves during this stage—and that will only get worse if we try to carry out a top-notch search without proper preparation.

Try to remind yourself that being in the process of finding your next job does not reduce your value as a person. Then will yourself off of that "safe" easy chair and get out there and do it!

➤

Distinguish between "forest," "tree," or "bark" personalities in your job hunt.

Forest people are quick, articulate, and results-oriented individuals who usually have good—or sometimes manipulative—interpersonal skills. Since they think quickly, they get bored easily and love new challenges. Forest people are people people; most need people around them to know who they are. If you compliment them, they glow.

They hate being tied to a desk for any length of time unless they are totally absorbed in what they are doing. They dislike detail. They either delegate very well or quickly do it themselves. They are often late unless they make an effort. Because this big picture or forest person can walk into a situation and quickly see what needs to be done, they often look brighter than others. It's no surprise that we often end up calling them boss.

When you are dealing with this kind of individual while seeking employment, follow-up often; they have so many things going on in their minds that they tend to forget things. They are flexible and rules-are-for-other-people thinkers, sometimes with obvious egos. Typical forest professions are sales, management of large staffs, negotiation, and all entrepreneurial positions. They are fired for taking too many liberties or threatening their insecure employers with change.

Tree people are a mixture of both forest (big picture) people and bark (detailed) people. Usually, however, they aren't as ready to accept change as forest people are and they handle detail better. They usually have reasonably good, although quieter, people skills. In other words, they are a mixture of the two ends of the scale. The majority of us fit into this classification. (I consider myself a tall tree, say a redwood.)

Bark personalities are sequential thinkers who are *very* detail oriented. They seek certifications rather than results. They have a hard time making decisions and want to avoid confrontation because they often have the people skills of a cardboard box. They are usually quiet with more thing skills than people skills. Most are self-involved and need a lot of personal attention from their boss. They want to know exactly how a task is to be performed. But if you compliment them they often think, "What does he want from me?"

They are logical and rational, organized and conscientious. They are self-critical, perfectionistic, and get caught up in the details, often failing to use initiative. They usually seek a nine-to-five job with very few incursions on their free time. Bark people are the last to leave a sinking company because they hate change so much. They are often fired because they are too slow.

Some of the best jobs for bark people are engineering, computer programming, editing, contract law, accounting, legal assistance, and scientific research—all places where their ability to organize and handle detail are assets.

If you're dealing with a bark employer during a job hunt, he or she will want a written resume and will not want you to bug him with lots of follow-up calls, despite the fact that he or she typically has a difficult time making decisions (read: taking risks). ➤

Protect your self-confidence by setting out to interview the employers.

Because you have a goal, you have more self-confidence. Psychologically, this is also a real boost to being attractive to companies, as well as protective of your own ego.

As always, do everything possible to insure that *you* are in control; don't leave your job future in a stranger's hands. ➤

Be persistent: try to check on decisions without waiting to be called.

Persistence, without being a pest, is what gains people jobs. You can write a thank-you note directly following the interview, then make two or three telephone calls. Should the decision still be delayed (it always seems to take twice as long as the employer indicates it will), send tidbits from trend news applicable to their business on your stationery.

(I track trends not only for my speaking engagements, but also so I have plenty of printed factual material on hand for my private clients.) ➤

Control yourself enough to

decide to do something, not

just research or continuously

change your resume.

I call people who overresearch "hummers," because they hum along but never learn to sing. You've got to get out and make those telephone calls and in-person visits.

Look to your past to give yourself the confidence that you can do it again. Know yourself, your skills, and your history. Know what makes you good at what you do; be able to talk about it.

Most important of all, *remind yourself* that you have these proficiencies—then *act!* ➤

Seriously consider helping others while you help yourself, particularly if you are already unemployed.

When you are home all day pursuing your quest for employment on your own, keeping self-motivated and directed can become quite a task as the weeks lengthen into months. So think about giving some time to others in greater need. This accomplishes a number of important things very quickly.

First, and most important, you'll feel good about making a difference in someone else's life. Clients of mine have tutored the underprivileged, volunteered at halfway houses, been eyes for the visually impaired, and taught English as a second language.

Second, you'll make contacts that can often prove to be very productive! Remember, networking is the way most jobs are landed.

Third, the shift in emphasis from *self* to *others* will help you to keep on truckin'. ➤

New Way #217

Listen to your voice on tape.

This will help you find out whether it is pleasant. Do you finish sentences? Do you sound like a whiner? Is your accent a deficit?

Make changes where necessary. For instance, I found that I speak rapidly without good inflection—too much a monotone—and dull. So I worked at changing it. And I now sound much better—a real asset in phone contacts, I can assure you! ➤

New Way #218

Expect dark little thoughts to creep into your mind.

There will be some unpleasantness as part of your emotional territory when you look for work. These ideas are capable of destroying your self-confidence. Knowing that it is common to job hunters to feel this way should go a long way toward banishing such goblins. ➤

Understand what's happening if you feel you are nothing because you aren't employed.

This is more particularly a disease of middle-aged males because, as we have noted, we are a culture in which males are raised to work.

The pressure to find a job increases tremendously when you don't have one, and you're apt to take the wrong one in a panic. Just as everyone has always told you, it *is* easier to change jobs when you already have one, because you are working from a position of ego strength.

Stay cool, calm, and collected. You're still you; use that you to hunt for something new. ➤

Grasp the idea that if you are resistant to change you are going to find a job hunt tough.

Flexibility is the name of the job hunt and career game today. But approximately eighty percent of the U.S. population, to greater or lesser degree, *resist* change by instinct.

Fear of making changes causes many people to research jobs but never really to *do* anything about them. All that free-floating anxiety that attends a new environment is more than some can overcome.

Please don't find yourself in the position of the perfectionist who must do it right, and so rarely does anything at all. Since you spend most of your waking hours working, you deserve to be employed in a reasonably enjoyable area. ➤

Understand that you cannot
overstress yourself.

For heaven's sake, if you can help it, don't make another major life change at the same time you're job hunting.

Changes like marriage, moving, going through a divorce, or having a child are extremely stressful. You're asking for real physical or mental trouble if you try to do too many of these things at once. ➤

Appreciate the fact that patience is required when waiting to hear whether you are accepted or rejected following a productive interview.

Potential employers have many reasons that have nothing to do with you for not getting back post haste. In fact, the higher level the job, the longer it usually takes for a decision to be made. You may be dealing with a company whose hiring practices are a bureaucratic horror; it may take months to do anything about hiring *anyone*. The budget may have been slashed, forcing decision makers to wait to see if the money to bring you on board is forthcoming. The company may suddenly be in a buyout mode, or have to freeze all hiring until organizational changes are made.

Then there are reasons that have to do with you more personally. Perhaps all the hiring authorities or managers can't agree on a candidate. This may be an internal political fight; employing you could be another example of power struggles that cross a number of lines.

So while you are doing everything you can to follow-up nicely, you should continue to actively seek work elsewhere—in fact, as *many* elsewheres as possible. ➤

Learn to deal positively with
rejection.

Never internalize rejection as failure on your part. You will hear *no* much more often than *yes* so expect it and try not to get your ego involved. Most markets are difficult today, so the Theory of Twenty-One we looked at earlier, which says it may take twenty-one calls before you make one sale, may become the Theory of Thirty (or Forty)! Job hunting is often ego smashing, frustrating, and thoroughly difficult. Don't take rejection personally. ➤

Relax and take your time in the interview.

Until you can feel worthwhile and powerful on your own, pretend that it is John Wayne attending the interview. Take your time, as the Duke would. Pause at the door and at the seat; the more time you take, the more status the other person will think you have.

This approach has its limits, of course—no one is suggesting taciturn belligerence at the interview—but the general idea should get you going in the right direction. ➤

New Way #225

Stay positive.

Think of what you want to accomplish today; make a list so you can mark off each task as it is completed. Use visualization to see yourself doing it, and get going.

If you are actively pursuing what you want to accomplish each day, you won't have time for fear to invade your mind. Either you master fear or it quickly masters you. Get started *now*! The longer you put things aside, the more dreaded they will become. ➤

New Way #226

Be flexible.

Often our original job goal will be altered by changing circumstances. Stay alert to opportunities you never thought about. As mentioned earlier, think about contract or consulting work and finding a niche for yourself while working inside on a part-time basis. Surveys have indicated that up to twenty-five percent of new jobs are part time, seasonal, contract, consulting, or temporary.

Don't work against this trend if it makes sense for you to work *with* it! ➤

Make decisions now.

Did you know that the longer it takes you to make a decision, the more difficult it becomes?

A friend of mine, after the downturn in the Texas oil industry, looked for new employment a while, found nothing he liked, and promptly dropped out. He now fills his days with God knows what, while his wife (aided by a little family money) supports them. He justifies all this with the zeal of the born-again Christian rejecting the heathen world. What a waste of wonderful gifts because of perfectionistic fears! ➤

Study the idea of soliciting funds for a scholastic, religious, charitable, artistic, or political group as a means of widening your acquaintances.

Volunteer fundraisers are always welcome for church groups, for cancer, heart, and other disease prevention societies, for your alumni group, or for private schools.

Rather than think of this as something to skip town to avoid, join in and make new friends . . . and widen your network of potential job sources while you do something worthwhile. This type of activity is especially appropriate for those seeking a career in sales! ➤

Realize that job hunting is a
full-time job.

Work hard at it, and things will begin to happen. Get up, get dressed, start making calls, writing letters, and mailing notes. Keep a day-by-day schedule book. Document calls and put callbacks in your daily agenda.

Exercise daily—take a walk in the evening to quiet your nerves and to drain the adrenaline so you can relax. ➤

Understand that you must be available and be easy to get in touch with.

It bears repeating: You or your telephone recorder must be reachable. I've known several people to miss good opportunities because they simply couldn't be found! Enlist friends or associates is you have to. I've taken calls for a client who was down on his luck financially after a divorce, had to move while seeking work, and had no telephone. He was out all day searching, and our office number became his phone number since someone was always there. He called in twice a day. He found a management job in three weeks! ➤

Find your own job and your
confidence will soar.

You'll love yourself when you have done all this and found a job. It is wonderful to feel you did it all by yourself, and you did it well. No greater self-confidence boost is imaginable. Next time (and there will probably be a next time in this convulsive economy) you will find it one-tenth as difficult! ➤

Read these job-hunting

experiences to be prepared.

An experienced church professional shared in writing some job-hunting experiences that had happened in the years prior to her consulting me. See if you can see other approaches that would have made her reaction to losing work less painful. The brackets are my comments.

"My first step was to rework my resume. I wrote a job description, listed functional skills, cataloged statements regarding the experiences used to fulfill the above objective, listed job experiences, education, and present references.

"Second, I wrote a cover letter that would introduce who I was personally . . . and professionally. . . . I was specific. [Remember, cold mailouts have a little less than a fifteen-hundred-to-one chance of finding you a job!]

"Third, I contacted my references. I asked if they would send a letter of recommendation that I could include with the above information.

"Fourth, I now was ready to contact institutional placement offices. I asked them to send me their vacancy list. They encouraged me to fill out their forms. They sent these forms with the vacancy lists. I looked at the forms and thought, this will make my being unique impossible, and if I send them this form, they will control who gets it. I decided to tell the placement office that I had to move quickly so as to be a good steward of Mother's money [the small inheritance she was counting on while hunting work]. The placement office encouraged me to try! I looked over the forms and my materials. I felt I had covered the required basic information. I looked at the vacancy list, selected fifteen institutions where I felt I could live and ones whose salary matched my needs. [Rarely does one find a job through a placement office of *any kind*.]

"Fifth, I had my materials copied professionally on bond paper and put them in an attractive folder. A word of advice— even professional typists make mistakes. If you can't proof the copy, take the extra time to get professional proofing. Mine was sent out with typographical errors that I only now am catching. [Good advice.]

"My first packets were mailed in late January to fifteen institutions and believe me, when I dropped them into the mail slot it was done with a spirit of hope. [If you recall the chances of gaining employment through this cold mailout method is 1 in 1,477.]

"February came and I was not enjoying the waiting. The Protestant work ethic within me intensified my need for work. I applied for part-time office work and I worked two nights a week at a florist and gift shop.

"As March blew in so did despair. I was not prepared for what I had to face. I was confronted with receiving no responses. *My way* seemed like a complete flop. Then two responded, but they wrote that the positions were *filled*. Another called to say the same, yet he encouraged me to continue my search. He was impressed with my materials. The other twelve didn't even have the courtesy to acknowledge receipt of my information. [Don't expect it.] To me that was inexcusable! I screamed with anger . . . didn't my fellow professionals know that my efforts represented two months of hard work and $200 I could hardly afford? [She wanted things to happen quickly, but three months for an entry-level position is average, and she was very experienced, so it might be expected to take much longer.]

"April blossomed into June, during which time I made local inquiries. I interviewed for several positions and felt like the prophet . . . "unwelcomed in my own land." [She expected religious institutions to treat her with more kindness than business people . . . not necessarily so; bureaucracies are the same everywhere!]

So: my part-time jobs were not generating enough, I had at this point cashed $2,000 of Mother's stock, and I was no closer to my goal . . . in fact I was back to zero! [Not really; she had found out what does not work . . . all that mailing out stuff in the traditional manner. Of course, she *was* keeping our postal system afloat!]

"Sixth, I wrote and called friends to pray that I would get a job by September. [The best thing she's done so far: contacted friends, but she should also have given them some more concrete ways to help!]

"Seventh, I talked [the placement offices] into giving me vacancy information before it was published. They gave me a list of five. I even spent a week calling institutional executives to ask if they knew of any job openings. This proved fruitless. [But she was starting to get on the right track . . . now dealing through people . . . but perhaps not enough of them or the right kind.]

"July passed. The August heat penetrated the house because my budget did not allow for air conditioning. I went to the owner of the florist/gift shop and I asked 'Would you consider me as a commercial sales representative? I know I can get corporate accounts.' He answered, 'I will consider you as manager of my year-round Christmas Shop and I'll talk about pursuing commercial accounts when I return from the Dallas Market September 15.' I went home that evening with new hope. I did my chores that night with new energy instead of my usual fatigue." [She had finally realized that *everything happens through people*, and began to understand she was already in a place to make something happen. Maybe not what she had originally planned, but personal flexibility is the key in a convulsive economy.]

Not long after that, due to her new approach, she was contacted and hired for a job in her professional area. ➤

New Way #233

Be sure you are memorable.

Follow up after the interview to outmaneuver your competition, and (ready for a piece of revolutionary advice?) show that you still retain some manners. This is often more than enough to make you stand out! ➤

New Way #234

Be sure your thank-you notes
are perfect.

Make sure names are correctly spelled with proper titles. A note places your name in front of decesion makers again, reminds them of your interest, and makes you stand out as that rare individual who takes the trouble to write one. In the note remind your interviewers of qualifications that seemed to spark their interest, and ask a question that will become an excuse for a later follow-up telephone call. Ask about *what more you can do to qualify for the job.* ➤

Beware of waiting for "the call".

Telephone after your note and prior to the date that was indicated as the decision deadline (but remember, that rarely turns out to be correct; however, it's usually twice as long). Learn to nag *nicely* by calling two or three times for status checks.

If they begin to ignore your calls, then you can send trend articles "they might have missed" about their business.

Another tactic for gaining a promised interview after several telephone calls was employed by one of my brighter clients. The prospective interviewer had teased her about her good vocabulary. After many attempts and cancelled meetings, she sat down with her dictionary and proposed a meeting time in a letter written in the most high-flown, verbose style she could muster. He called back, laughing, and immediately set up a meeting time.

These sorts of strategies continually remind your prospective employer that you exist. If you consider this tactful persistence overbearing, you are unrealistic about the kind of time the decision makers usually have to think about hiring. They will more likely consider the calls, notes, and articles an indication of career direction than rudeness. ➤

Elbow your way onto the short list—tactfully.

If you find the interviewer is not placing you among the top candidates, make an effort to elbow your way onto the short list. Don't just sit there and let things happen to you! Respond to objections. Highlight strengths and employer benefits with polite tenacity. What have you got to lose? ➤

Persuade with other assets should your education or experience qualifications be lacking.

Emphasize how intense, even if short, your variety of experience has been. "I know some people can stay in a job for years and do not have the experience I have. With my enthusiasm (or loyalty) you could look for months and find no one who will more quickly become an efficient economic asset."

To compensate for a lack of formal education say, "I have been successfully competing with people who have degrees for several years. I'm results-oriented and that seems to be what most employers want when it comes to the bottom line." Or, "By the time I could afford to go to college, I was already doing the job I would have studied to do, and successfully competing with people with two degrees!" ➤

Feel that your age—too old or too young—is a deficit?

Remind the interviewer how old President Reagan was when he took office! Or that Mozart was composing music when he was a child of eight, and had completed music's most magnificent career by his mid-thirties.

Age means different things to different people. George Burns, in his nineties, is still performing on TV, and George Bernard Shaw was still producing plays at that age. George Blanda was still playing football in his forties, but Mickey Mantle was twenty when he hit twenty-three home runs. Everyone remembers that Grandma Moses was in her eighties before even *beginning* to paint. Enthusiasm and talent are what matter, not chronological age!

Do understand, however, that when you are past fifty, you often run into problems because the retirement numbers make it more difficult for a company to hire you. Simply mention that you are flexible about working out retirement plans if that issue seems to be a problem. ➤

Do this if you are told you're
too experienced.

This usually means too expensive or too old.

Say, "My experience may *seem* to cost more, but I also become productive immediately, making up for money spent on long training periods required by a less experienced person. I'm dedicated to my field, ambitious, and healthy. And I cannot imagine retirement at this point in my life!" ➤

Be prepared to cite

---

accomplishments that have

---

allowed you to be paid well if

---

the prospective employer says

---

he can't afford you.

The company will get more than ordinary value for the salary. Over and over I've seen companies make all sorts of creative salary arrangements to hire the person they want, even placing people in the retirement program who were approaching sixty! Could they consider perhaps expanding your duties to justify the salary?

Ask! ➤

New Way #241

Counter with what you consider to be the attributes of your leading contender.

Having now understood the needs of the organization, this is an excellent time to compose and deliver an employment proposal based on the "advantages" you may feel a competitor is showcasing to good effect (see chapter 9). You need to let this employer know what you can do to make or save the company money! ➤

New Way #242

Project a confident, open, phone image.

Remember to be enthusiastic. It's hard to build rapport with a zombie!

After all, if you're on the phone with a prospective employer, your voice is the only image he has to judge you by. Make sure it's the right image! ➤

Be sure to keep in touch if you were one of the first people interviewed.

This is especially important if they say they will interview many people before making a decision. You *have to* keep in touch because the more people interviewed, the harder their decision will be. Let them know you want the job, but need to know quickly (because of another offer, for instance).

Try *not* to be the first interviewed. ➤

Stand out from the crowd.

Send things by overnight mail, or have a friend carry the information in for you. A firm will often give offers to people with less-than-wonderful qualifications if the firm thinks the employee *really* wants the job.

Sending letters and resumes the traditional ways mean that you will be processed through traditional channels. Recently one of my clients landed a pharmaceutical sales position after having been in women's retail clothing sales. How? She initially interviewed for advice, and was liked, but was rejected because of her lack of direct sales experience. The client then sent a relevant article (the first was "How to Sell to Doctors") to the decision maker once a month for eight months—until she was hired! ➤

Keep from going bonkers during a job hunt by being realistic about how long it takes to get a job.

So many people think that all you have to do is cut out a few ads, mail off some resumes, contact a personnel agency, or make a few phone calls, and you'll have a job in a couple of weeks. If it doesn't happen, you get depressed and quit or rewrite and rewrite your resume (as if that will get you a job)!

That attitude simply denies the real facts about the national averages for finding employment, which, we must remember, are that it takes three months to find an entry-level position. For every notch you are up on the ladder, add more time. (The conventional wisdom is one month for every ten thousand in salary.) For an upper-level manager, one year or longer is not unrealistic, unless you are in a high-demand business. ➤

Plan each day in order to keep
your cool.

Keep on doing things to market yourself *despite* the rejection of yesterday or that feeling of nervous nothingness (free-floating anxiety). Write lists and teach yourself to use them. Train yourself to feel successful if everything on your list has been marked off by day's end. Enough contacts and list writing, and eventually things will begin to break your way! ➤

Exercise to keep your
enthusiasm and sanity.

If you are a results-oriented person who seeks change and wants to make things happen now, you will probably become very frustrated by the fact that you cannot get a job today, if not yesterday! When that happens you cannot relax, so sleep is interrupted. Try going for a walk after your evening meal, so you can relax.

If, however, you tend to be the kind of person who goes out to lunch alone, happily, and you love just being by yourself in a corner, then you may start to hide out at home and quit seriously seeking employment except by the most impersonal of means. You would really like someone to do it for you because you don't feel in control. What you need to do, and sometimes it is the most difficult thing on earth, is to drag yourself off the sofa or out of bed and do something really sweaty to release endorphins. Then you can get back to doing what you *need* to do to make a job happen for yourself—contact people.

Feel in control again by reading motivational books such as *Pulling Your Own Strings* by Dr. Dwayne Dyer. ➤

Avoid people who are downers.

These people can include parents and spouses!

Surround yourself with the most positive people you know, and be open with them. If those around you are nagging, give them something constructive to do to aid you in your hunt, such as making phone calls or doing some research. This will at least give them some perspective on what you're going through! ➤

Consider these measures if you've been out of work so long you've totally lost your self-confidence.

1. *Get up off that chair* (or bed) and go for a brisk walk.

2. *Go to your local library* or bookstore and borrow or buy motivating tapes or books. What most of these books and tapes say is that you are in control, and when you really believe that, you can act.

3. *Let your mind see this as a new challenge*, instead of replaying all the hurts of being unemployed. I know this can be difficult, but if you cannot accomplish it, you will only hurt yourself.

4. *Find a kind listener* and ask for help in finding leads (once *you* have decided the areas in which you will look).

5. *Pamper yourself.* Bring yourself to look your very best. Keep in mind how important image is in getting and keeping a job.

6. *Find a temporary job or consulting work* that gets you out with people. You will not find a career position by hiding out at home.

7. *Think flexibly.* Would you move? How about trying two different directions at once.

8. *Reset goals, and break them into daily doables.* You must use your time wisely, or you will accomplish nothing.
➤

Heed these basic thinking
errors when job hunting.

We often worry about the big *what ifs*; those things that may never happen. This kind of inflexible detail-oriented thinking leads to job-hunting anxiety, which all of us have a touch of from time to time. I consider paranoia almost normal in a job hunter.

This following is from the Phobia Society of America. Job hunt examples in brackets are by my firm, Hour Savers.

1. **All or nothing thinking**—the tendency to see things in extremes. ["I know this is the last chance I'll ever have to find a job in my field."]

2. **Overgeneralization**—selecting a single negative event as a continuous, unending pattern of defeat. ["That interview was pure agony and my responses were just plain dumb. I will never, ever interview well."]

3. **Mental filter**—selecting a single negative detail and dwelling on it exclusively. ["I wouldn't have been laid off if George hadn't had it in for me."]

4. **Disqualifying the positive**—thinking that positive aspects of a situation don't count. ["Although I learned more at my last job than one could possibly learn in ten years of school, since I don't have a degree I'll never find another decent job."]

5. **Jumping to conclusions**—making a negative interpretation without any facts to support your conclusion. ["Since I have no experience in that field, I will never be able to find work there."]

6. **Catastrophizing**—exaggerating the importance and consequences of events and assuming that the worst will happen. ["Because I was fired, I know I'll never be able to find another job."]

7. **Should statements**—using words such as *should*, *shouldn't*, *must* and *ought* as a way to punish and pressure yourself and others. ["I should have quit months ago; now I'm in a situation where I must have the perfect job within three months."]

9. **Labeling and mislabeling**—attaching a negative label to yourself and others rather than describing specifically bothersome behavior. ["I was dumb to stay so long with those losers."]

10. **Personalization**—to see yourself as the total cause of some negative occurrence for which you were not primarily responsible (as children often do in divorce). ["I wouldn't be looking for work today if I'd spoken up about the Hobbs contracts; I'm sure that's why our company was not doing well."] ➤

Know when to seek professional
psychological help.

If you find yourself frequently thinking or making statements like the negative self-talk in New Way #250, you are not controlling yourself emotionally. The wise person, at this point, hunts help.

You're too valuable to waste! Take the time to get some counseling if this is in order. ■

Chapter 14

Negotiate Your New Salary

I make my job-hunt seminar attendees stand and swear, with arms upraised, that they will never reveal an exact salary amount, past or present, on any form or in any interview until the interviewer has first showed his/her hand! Whenever you do so, you have really painted yourself into a corner.

You, too, can become a good salary negotiator, so let's spend some time thinking about handling the delicate issue of pay and benefits. Self-confidence without cockiness, along with lots of practice, will help you find that job with a good salary. But, you must believe you deserve to be paid. Asking for too little can be as damaging to your cause as asking for too much. ➤

Play your cards right: stall until the last to discuss salary.

All your efforts up until now should have been directed at filling *the employer's* needs. In fact, I've put this section near the end of the book because I'm hoping that will help you remember to stall until the last to discuss this touchy issue.

The rule is a simple one. The longer and more often you sit in that interview seat, the stronger your negotiating stance becomes.

➤

Attempt to discover what the average salaries are in your field.

Call and talk with friends, people who hold the same position in other companies, or a Human Resources Consultant or Personnel Department in a similar company to see what are the usual salaries for the job. Then you may simply want to plan on aiming for a percentage more than your present salary, or decide what you must make in order to live! Be realistic. In a tough market, your competition may come cheaper. ➤

Do not put yourself in a box by writing or stating salary wanted or presently earned.

It bears repeating. On forms and applications, just leave present and past salaries blank or draw a line through them; those figures are used as screening devices. If the form asks how much salary you expect, write *negotiable* (they'll figure you're reasonably well educated if you can spell it properly). Tell them, with a smile, that you will be willing to discuss salary when they've gotten to know you, and you them, and everyone is seriously interested. Period. Smile.

If Human Resources/Personnel clerks (these are the people who are most uptight about salary history) still insist those little salary boxes be filled out, simply tell them you'll be glad to discuss salary with the decision maker should an offer be made. And smile. And pray. ➤

Be ready for "What kind of money are you looking for?"

The usual way an interviewer will approach talking about salary is by saying, "What kind of money are you looking for?" "What are you making now?," or, "How much would it take you to live?"

If salary is brought up early in your interviews, simply say, "I'd like to delay talking about that until I know you better and you know me. Then I'm sure we'll be able to work something out." Or as one of my favorite male clients (now president of a company) said, "I'd really like to delay discussing salary; I like to peel an onion one layer at a time." Then smile! (By the way, he got that job.)

The decision maker thinks that if what you earn now or what you ask is far too low, then obviously you are incompetent to do a job with the responsibilities of this one. If your asking price is too high, you're beyond their salary levels. Most prospective employers will try to find out what you're making and offer you a little more. However, the final offer needs to be in line with what someone of comparable responsibility is being paid in their firm already. ➤

Don't commit to anything until the interviewer commits to a salary range.

Delay as long as possible talking about salary, company cars, vacations, medical, and retirement benefits. The longer you stall, the more attractive your negotiating posture will usually be.

Try these stalling ploys to make the interviewer commit to a salary range: "I'm sure you pay good people well, and I know you'll include me among those good people." Or, "It would be presumptuous to name a figure now; let's wait until the organization is sure it likes me, and I it, then see what we can work out."

Or, if all else fails, just keep smiling and saying things like, "I'm sure you have a salary tied to this position." ➤

Look at this real-life example
of negotiating salary.

My client, Robert, had been working for a firm with a reputation for poor salaries. However, because young Robert had a wonderful in-house (though terribly underpaid) mentor, he quickly became known for a superior quality of work. Robert was approached by another corporation with more mainstream hiring and salary practices.

My advice to Robert, who wasn't particularly articulate but had a great presence (he was a handsome six feet, four inches tall), was to not reveal any salary history or the new company would think he was unqualified, given the low salary he was presently making. He was to nod a lot, look the interviewer in the eye, smile, and say, "I'm sure you have a salary tied to this position," and absolutely nothing else on the topic.

Robert reported that he said that phrase three times, and little else, during the salary negotiations. In fact, he let silence rule until the interviewer stated a salary range. In true bazaar fashion, Robert went higher, so the interviewer could negotiate him down, setting up a win-win situation. Robert was hired on the spot and offered 42% more than he had been earning! ➤

Remember to stall and qualify

during negotiations.

You are attempting to do the same thing the interviewer is—to determine an equitable salary for you. Your move is to say little and continue to throw the ball back to the interviewer's court.

The person who speaks most here, loses! ➤

Force the interviewer to reveal

the salary first, then top it.

You can come down and they can come up, creating a win-win situation. If the interviewer says, "Well, we planned this job to be in the low thirties," you say, "I was expecting at least $38,000." Then hope to get $35,000. ➤

Negotiate perks, if you can't negotiate a good salary, but see lots of promise in the position.

These perks could include car allowances, special insurance packages, early vesting in retirement programs, or even, if all else fails, reviews of salary and performance at three and six months (especially in a smaller company, where it is often difficult to be reviewed at all).

One of my clients in the financial area found a challenging opening with great potential but failed to budge the rather rigid salary offer. My client indicated, with a smile, that the salary offered was at least $5,000 below the area average for his experience and education. He was told to take the original offer or leave it! Not only that, my client was then told he must save his own salary within the company the first year to make it worth hiring him!

There was too much opportunity in this high-growth company to let the chance pass, so my client accepted the low salary but negotiated a written promise of reviews of his salary and performance at three and six months. Within three months he had already saved his salary and received another 11 percent. More importantly, he was labeled the company's fast-track kid, and the CEO told him how much he would probably be earning at the end of two years! That figure was more than my client would have dreamed. ➤

New Way #261

Realize that many women, in particular, have trouble negotiating salary.

I think this has something to do with the cultural hangover of not feeling worthy of earning real money.

I attended a business banquet and was seated next to a male banker who declared during the course of the evening—after three or four glasses of wine—that he loved hiring women. I asked why. He said, "Because they never negotiate salary." Take that as a warning, working women! We will get what we ask for and expect. ➤

Note this story of a woman
negotiating salary.

A client named Kelly was highly qualified in all phases of the travel industry. She had grown up in the business and worked in travel agencies, hotels, and had been a major city convention director. After airline deregulation, she had been employed by two companies that had closed their doors during those troubled times. Finally she'd taken the only thing available—with a small commuter airline for $12,500 a year!

Kelly was an assertive, articulate person. She was so vivacious that she could tire you out from sheer enthusiasm. She was apt to reveal her salary just because she talked a lot. I told Kelly, who eventually was called to the West Coast to interview with a major tour company, that she was to be quiet, mirror the body language of the person to whom she was talking, keep her hands still, smile and say, "I'm sure you have a salary tied to this position," when asked about salary history.

Kelly, who called me from the interview site to go over last-minute instructions, came home with a fantastic job, a base salary of $35,000, plus a commission, a car, and all travel expenses paid. Do you really think, if the interviewer had known she was earning $12,500, that they would have made those arrangements?
➤

Be aware that the easier you are to get, the less you'll be valued.

That is one of the major troubles with many women; they are so nice and helpful that it never even occurs to them to negotiate salary.

Remember, even if you lose all your negotiating points and you end up accepting the salary and benefits offered, you still have set into the decision maker's mind the fact that you must be dealt with in the future if he intends to keep you. So, negotiating is always a winning tactic. If you don't get immediate results, you will often find later on that it has paid in quicker raises or promotions. ➤

Use one job offer to force another prospective employer's hand.

Call and tell them you've gotten an offer from ABC but would rather work for them. They'll let you know if they're interested right away! ➤

Try these ideas after you have
an offer.

Stall again. Say, "Mr. Jones, I have promised to attend another interview, as well as discuss any job offers with my husband/wife/mentor. I am excited and enthusiastic about your offer, but I want to make a rational decision. I'll give you my formal acceptance within the week (or whatever time period is right for you), and work out a time to start shortly afterwards."

Tell the interviewer that this is an important career decision, and you want to be totally certain before you resign your present position.

Then call people who know about this company. You might ask the interviewer or Personnel for a couple of names of past employees you can contact. Be wary if they have trouble thinking of past employees who would vouch for them. Call these names, and call other people in the field who will be able to tell you more about the organization. ➤

Try to get a salary offer in
writing.

For what it's worth in these days of revolutionary changes in business practices, get your job offer in writing as to title, salary, benefits, and any other things promised. This can prevent you from becoming one of the many sad people who did not receive what was verbally promised.

Declining in writing sometimes gains you a better offer, too!

■

Chapter 15

Select from Offers

How do you logically decide to take a job offer? Even with only one offer, there is a time-tested decision-making process that can coolly and unemotionally give you some direction by analyzing your own feelings. Respond to those questions that are relevant to your particular situation. ➤

Try this process to help you decide if you should seriously consider your new offer(s):

Assign from a *10* (highest), down to *0* (lowest) in answer to the following questions for each job offer.

1. Does it make use of my aptitudes and work style? Does it make me feel successful and happy most of the time?

2. Is this job leading toward my ultimate goal or goals?

3. Does my research made through those who know the organization make me feel comfortable with this job?

4. Do I identify with the kind of people who work there?

5. Is this a thriving industry, an Information Age business?

6. Does my offer include good benefits, perks, bonuses?

7. Does this job provide flexibility? Is it not tied to a desk or rigid hours?

8. Do I perceive the job as secure? Are there few layoffs? (Harder and harder to find after the demise of womb-to-tomb employment.)

9. Does it promise money, now or later?

10. Do I find it challenging with much variety?

11. Is there responsibility, a chance to be on the management fast track?

12. Will my spouse be able to find a similar opportunity should we relocate?

13. Does the offer compensate for change in economic or living standards?

14. Can I place a value on staying in familiar surroundings, near friends or family, in your hometown?

15. Are the hours good?

16. Does it provide status or a pleasant working environment?

17. Is it located where I want to be? ➤

Having answered the prior questions, now try to logically rank your present job alongside your offer(s).

The firm with the highest number will win you as part of their team.

There is one warning you should bear in mind before accepting: you should know whether leaving your present job is a logical move. If your offer isn't a considerable improvement over your present employment, perhaps you need to keep on looking.

➤

Realize that there is no
perfect job.

Realize that the best offers go to enthusiastic—not gushy—people who want to work for the company and who like the job, the interviewer, and life in general!

You will realize by the end of the interviewing process, just as during the initial building of rapport, that attitude and personality outweigh qualifications and education tremendously. ∎

Chapter 16

Take Action

Still having trouble? Try the following steps to give yourself a jump start! ➤

New Way #270

Get going!

Try setting your kitchen timer to force you to really begin to do those three things that you dread, whatever they are (usually making telephone calls).

Face it: You will *never* find a job hiding out at home! ➤

New Way #271

Know who you are and what you want, and be able to talk about it in broad terms.

Not: "I want to make a lot of money," or, "I want to work a forty-hour week without stress". Say, "My goal is to be an accountant." "I have three areas in which my qualifications would fit—Executive Assistant/Office Manager, Customer Service/Sales Support, or Personnel/Human Resources." "I am a Career and Employment Consultant."

What abilities and skills do you really have? Make sure you have not forgotten all the relevant military or special courses you have taken, in addition to regular formal schooling. Know your immediate and long-term goals. ➤

Remember that resumes are simply a support to your professionalism.

I repeat: resumes are not that all-important item on which your career rests. Telephone calls and personal contacts are tremendously more important than simple pieces of paper. ➤

Forget trying to produce the perfect resume.

There isn't one. Just make sure it is eye catching, the spelling is correct, and it isn't sloppy, too short, too long, or dull. ➤

New Way #274

Be out among people all you can.

Talk about what you are doing. Take or send a resume later, if needed. This is much more productive than mailing resumes. ➤

New Way #275

Enlist friends.

Make it a rule never to mail a resume until all other avenues to the decision maker have been blocked.

That means you never mail a resume until you have attempted to enlist *every single one of your friends* who could conceivably help you. ➤

Do research and understand that knowledge is power!

Know yourself, each prospective company and interviewer beforehand. ➤

Review the basics often.

Practice job-hunting techniques that make you appear different in a nice way. Reread chapter 11. ➤

Keep an open mind.

As we have seen, it is necessary to throw away traditional job-hunting methods, which usually include answering ads, mailing to lists, responding to job banks, and going to private or public employment agencies. If you do these, don't expect much to happen. If it does, you are just plain lucky!

If you look like every other job hunter, sound like every other job hunter, and use the same methods as every other job hunter, why shouldn't potential employers treat you like every other job hunter? ➤

Use the following creative and tremendously productive methods.

It bears repetition. Everything, including finding employment, happens through people, not through a piece of paper.

1. Benefactoring or networking

2. Asking decision makers for a few minutes of time for some advice ➤

Understand that what you are
selling is smiling
self-confidence.

Try to project a nice mixture of self-assurance, warmth, and preparedness; these are the hallmarks of professionalism. ➤

Start an avalanche.

Know that if you can find one job lead, you can find lots more. If you changed jobs before and survived, you can do it again.

It really does get easier as you move ahead! ➤

Keep in mind still another reason to avoid personnel departments: your positive self-image.

I always tell my seminar attendees that if they are into whips and chains, they should go to Human Resources. These people will find things wrong with you that you never suspected! Remember . . .

1. If you don't fit their particular recipe or job description, its File 13—the wastebasket!

2. Even gaining the confidence of someone in Personnel/Human Resources does not always help much, because they are *not decision makers*.

3. Personnel is very often *unaware* of openings available within their own organization. I could cite case after case of clients who got jobs by directly approaching the decision maker, after having been screened out by Personnel more than once! ➤

Image is important, so be prepared to stow away the "real you" if necessary, at least for a while.

Image has almost everything to do with ultimate success. Remember, this is theater. Unfortunately, decision makers won't have time to look for the real you. So, if you have the mind-set today of the Sixties Child, you are in for a long job hunt. Can you afford to be old-fashioned and out of step with the times? ➤

Practice interviewing.

Be prepared, enthusiastic and interested. Interview often so you become comfortable doing so. Practice your interview skills before any interview. Rehearse answers about your abilities, work preferences, career goals, and personal qualities.

Surprisingly, many job hunters are foggy about the details of their own work history. Review dates of school and employments, your accomplishments, and skills you have learned.

Ask for rehearsal help from a family member or friend, or use a tape recorder or video camera. See yourself interviewing as you go to bed the night before, and you'll wake up knowing how to act and what to expect in your interview. ➤

Be assertive.

This doesn't mean that you should be aggressive. It means being confident of your abilities, and being able to get results when working with other people.

This trait will not only help you interview confidently; it will project a very positive job performance trait. ➤

Avoid personal issues.

Avoid such issues as family, religious, personal or financial problems. These issues have no place whatsoever at a job interview. ➤

New Way #287

Don't criticize.

Don't criticize your present or previous employers, teachers or co-workers. It will *always* reflect negatively on you.

Think of it from the employer's perspective. How would *you* react to someone who never had a good word for former supervisors and co-workers. ➤

New Way #288

Have something to offer the organization.

The interview is not complete unless the interviewer knows exactly how you can meet a need or solve a problem. Emphasize your strengths. Focus on experience, schooling, or personal qualities that will be beneficial for the job. Tell stories that illustrate examples from your experience or education. For more ideas, see the employment proposals in chapter 9. ➤

Collect work samples.

Bring these to interviews (or to send later as a follow-up device). This could be artwork, writing samples, news clips, publications, photographs, written reports, or technical drawings. ➤

The further up the scale you are looking, the longer it will take.

Unfortunately, rejection is an inescapable part of any job search, and you must be prepared to face it. The key is to not waste your time and energy feeling dejected, but to learn from the process. ➤

New Way #291

Remember to build rapport and
the Theory of Twenty-one.

Achieve that instant rapport in the first seconds of the interview. The Theory of Twenty-one states that it takes an average of twenty-one calls to make one sale. By combining these two steps, you will simultaneously better your odds and remind yourself that employment really is a numbers game. ➤

New Way #292

Keep plugging.

Read every word of the following paragraph.

There is no substitute for persistence! There is no substitute for persistence! There is no substitute for persistence! There is no substitute for persistence! There is no substitute for persistence! There is no substitute for persistence! There is no substitute for persistence! There is no substitute for persistence! There is no substitute for persistence! ➤

Maintain perspective.

Learn to back out, instead of forcing the issue when the rapport is not there. Don't try to get blood from a stone. Work with what's in front of you and know that the simple act of taking a systematic approach will set you apart from the vast majority of your competitors.

Laugh whenever you can. ➤

Review your own accomplishments.

Set short-term daily and weekly goals in order to feel successful in little things. Make five or ten calls per day; write ten notes or letters. Mark them off in your agenda book when they are completed. ➤

Follow up interviews with a thank-you letter, personal notes, and telephone calls.

Restate your interest in the job and summarize key points of the interview, or add further information to help your case along. If you have gone to all this time, trouble, and expense, don't give up now! You owe those who help you find leads a thank-you note, as well. Be politely assertive! ➤

Remember that job-hunting

expenses are often

tax-deductible.

For some insane reason known only to the IRS, you must be looking for work in the same field in which you are now engaged in order to take this deduction. So going to school to work toward your CPA when you have been a corporate sales trainer is not deductible. But money spent on this book, newspapers (for the employment sections), postage and mailings, career advice and testing, and driving (the standard government deduction), and transportation and housing out of town to interview (if not paid by the prospective employer) are all tax deductible. Document everything you do. (Of course, these deductions don't apply for the first-time job hunter.) ➤

New Way #297

Give yourself a break.

If you're taking yourself too seriously, drop everything and do something fun. Give yourself an hour of guilt-free pleasure; indulge in something you "never had the time" to do before.

I've done this by reading A.A. Milne's *The House at Pooh Corner*, jumping rope in private, and renting *Annie Hall*. Again. How about you? ➤

New Way #298

Understand yourself well enough to schedule your day the way that controls you best.

If you are a quick, results-oriented, and impatient personality, it may be wiser for you to go at the job hunt night and day for a few days, then take two or three days off. Other, more organized personalities, will be able to keep at it quietly day after day. ➤

Never, never give up, but do think flexibly.

Many of my clients today discover offers that they didn't even know existed when they began their job hunt. They also often turn contract or consulting jobs into full-time employment.

You can, too! ➤

Don't try to leap tall buildings in a single bound.

Take a step at a time. And remember, procrastination is usually a product of fear of the unknown. Even if your present job is a dead-end one and a drag on your psyche, you may decide to stay out of sheer inertia! Watch out for this cycle.

Reduce time-wasting by breaking the task into small segments that are not so daunting.

1. Research to find out who could use you. This means lots of reading and telephone calls.

2. Write your resume or employment proposal; you'll be able to talk about yourself.

3. List and contact friends and acquaintances for leads.

4. Follow-up on *all* leads until you have interviews.

5. Prepare for interviews carefully.

6. Follow-up on interviews with thank-you notes and some of the more creative methods listed in this book.

Good luck!